Nobody's Business

Toby Moffett

Nobody's Business

The Political Intruder's Guide to Everyone's State Legislature

Introduction by
Ralph Nader

The Chatham Press, Inc.
Riverside, Connecticut

ACKNOWLEDGEMENTS

If there had been no General Assembly Project there would, obviously, be no book. Therefore I wish to express my appreciation of their immeasurable efforts to my colleagues on the Project:

to Angie Martin and Marty Rogol, who have created the best state-wide citizen lobby in the country. Through their leadership and the persistence of three thousand CCAG citizen lobbyists this book—and the Project it describes—were made possible;

to Debbie Gottheil and Emily Thomson, who spent more than eighty hours a week researching, interviewing and, with patience and courage, stood by those mimeo machines for nearly four weeks;

to the other full-time staffers—none of whom was paid more than $30 a week—John Wancheck, who continues to handle consumer organization, Alexandra Woods, Jan Withey, Nancy Carroll, Paul Shapiro, Miriam Frum and Kathy Steinfeld. Tollie Miller and Francesca Jordan also devoted a good portion of their summer to the research effort.

My gratitude also to the typists, students and journalists—volunteers all—who edited, collated and did countless menial tasks with good humor and perseverance.

Special thanks go to my editors, Naomi Karp and Christine O'Shea, and to Gil Kelman, who provided valuable and generous advice on production and distribution of the profiles.

And to the hundreds of citizens across the state who lent assistance, their efforts are warmly acknowledged.   —T.M.

July, 1973

Manufactured in the United States of America

SBN 85699-080-9 (cloth edition)
SBN 85699-081-7 (paper edition)
Library of Congress Catalog Card Number: 73-83355

Permission to quote copyrighted material is acknowledged to publishers and authors as follows: *The New York Times*, May 21, 1972 © 1972 by The New York Times Company. Bantam Books Inc. for *The Sometimes Governments: A Critical Study of the 50 American Legislatures* Copyright © 1971 by the Citizens' Conference on State Legislatures, written by John Burns. *The Hartford Times, The New Haven Register, The Waterbury Republican, The Bridgeport Telegram* and other daily and weekly newspapers whose words make up parts of this book are also acknowledged with thanks.

Contents

Introduction

THIS BOOK is directed to all Americans who refuse to despair before they dare; who do not give up before they try.

Nobody's Business is not a tortuous excursus into the technical and legal labyrinth of state legislatures. Rather it is the story of how a group of highly motivated citizens undertook to produce profiles on every Connecticut state legislator standing for re-election in November, 1972. Never before in this country had there been prepared and publicly released such detailed descriptions and data about each individual legislator!

The project director and author, Toby Moffett, recounts in the most human, down-to-earth fashion the assembling of the study team and how each difficulty was overcome in pursuit of the completion of the profiles. As the first study of this kind, it illuminated how the impact of making such information public, which political systems try to keep secret, unorganized or difficult to obtain, can be expanded with additional experience and resources. The effect on citizen education, the media and the legislators themselves should interest anyone who used to believe that "you can't fight city hall."

For those susceptible to the constructive enthusiasm of vicarious transfer, there is more in this book than a wealth of important advice about how to do such a study while avoiding possible pitfalls from production to distribution. There is also reflected a spirit of community, of self-help and of creative improvisation to overcome hurdles and stretch to unexpectedly high levels of citizen endurance.

There are fifty other legislatures (49 states and Puerto Rico) which deserve study by the voters. In addition to profiles of legislators and their voting and participation records, such studies should delve into the legislative committees, relations between the legislative and executive branches, and other institutional aspects of these elective bodies. In doing so, citizens are more likely to discover what it is they don't like, what it takes to make it right. People count if people care, and those who care soon find out that democracy without citizen action is a slogan that rapidly becomes an expensive mockery of human rights and our society's future.

While there are some books you can't put down, this volume strives to make you unable to put yourself down. In a word, it wants to get you involved in investigating a very important institution in your lives—the state legislature. It wants to get you concerned enough about your power, your taxes and your legislature to launch a citizens' study of the men and women who are supposed to represent you. The more citizens who get under way in activities such as these described by Moffett, the easier it will become to shape a state legislature that clearly represents the public interest. In fact, people will be surprised to learn that progressive changes are not as difficult as they are thought to be when democracy is left for the other fellow to worry about.

—RALPH NADER
Washington, D.C.
July, 1973

FOREWORD

THE CIRCULAR Senate chamber is jammed. The wood paneled walls are half-hidden by spectators who have come too late to find seats. Others lean against the gleaming brass railings that separate the audience from the legislators— thirty-four men and two women enthroned on green plush-upholstered and high-backed chairs around a horseshoe table. It is hot; the air is smoky and smelly. The heavy wood and glass doors open and close as people enter, and the armed guard at the main door has given up asking for identification.

A short, heavy man laboriously moves toward the microphone below the Speaker's platform. With twisted arms he drags himself on crutches, the perspiration visible on his face and neck. His shirt collar is open, a discarded tie hangs from a jacket pocket. Someone hurries forward to adjust the microphone. With surprising expertise, the man manipulates his crutches while reaching for some papers in another pocket. He smoothes them against his breast and clears his throat.

"You may not believe it," he says, "but I'm happy to be alive."

He tells how he had almost not been born, how a doctor twenty years earlier had advised his mother to undergo an abortion, aware that her unborn child was imperfect, to say the least.

"But who was he to judge? How did he dare say who should live and who should die? And are we God that *we* should say?" He pulls himself fully erect on his crutches and looks into the faces of the people nearest to him.

Some smile back, a few wipe their eyes. Many glare at him angrily.

"You selfish s.o.b." one woman calls out. "How about your mother's feelings?"

The public hearing on SB 109, A Bill to Legalize Abortion, is under way.

State governments, unlike national and municipal, are not the stuff of which novels are made. Allen Drury put Washington, D.C. on the best seller lists; Mike Royko has analyzed Chicago's Daley administration; movies have been made about Mayor Jimmy Walker's New York; and Fiorello La-Guardia's New York was the subject of a Broadway play.

The fifty state legislatures hold powers which directly and personally influence our lives, and yet the fact that no one sees them as grist for the literary mills is hardly surprising. True, the states tell us when we can marry, on what grounds we may divorce, whether our sexual practices are legal, how qualified our medical doctors must be, whether we are eligible for welfare, what taxes we must pay and how they are to be spent. In addition, the states establish criminal codes under which we may be arrested, maintain the courts in which we are tried and supervise the prisons where we may languish or become rehabilitated.

In the end, the states tell us how we may dispose of our estates and how much our heirs may keep.

But who cares? How exciting can a legislature be that meets part-time (as most do), has little if any staff, offers few individual offices in which to keep files, pays its members next to nothing (thus ensuring the domination of those who can financially afford to be there—lawyers and other self-employed professionals), has too many committees with far too many members for efficiency and works in the ever-present shadow of the governor?

What attracts the eye and remains in the memory of the average citizen appears not to be the newspaper articles on tormented arguments about abortion reform or the abolition of capital punishment, but those columns reporting nit-picking nonsense such as the two-hour debate in the Missouri Capitol over the salary of its janitor, or the excitement in Boston when one legislator was caught casting a roll call vote for another, or in Hartford when a mini-skirted, red-haired reporter led a battle to permit women in the Hawaiian Room (an ugly, barely furnished room where male legislators and reporters occasionally ate lunch). This indicates how the state legislatures are viewed by their constituencies—as slightly ridiculous, inefficient and not worth the effort of filling with capable lawmakers. Those persons who at some time or another decided to partake of the public hearings or become involved in the legislative process tell bitter tales of sitting through hour after hour of testimony from special interest lobbyists and legislators while the public had little chance or time to speak. Others recollect organizing hundreds of citizens to show support for a bill, taking time off from jobs, hiring babysitters, gathering information on the measure, driving to the state capitol, searching endlessly for parking space, to finally arrive and to testify—only to discover that the bill has disappeared, never to come up for final discussion or a vote before the full legislature.

(There apparently is reason for the groaning heard among Washington architects of national social programs in education, health and housing when the Administration speaks of giving the states more power in these areas. "These federal programs were created because the states were not doing the job of caring for their people," comments a former official of the Office of Economic Opportunity.)

But neglect of the states and their legislators has clearly outweighed any unhappiness with them. Even during the active and turbulent 1960's, they were let off the hook. While most institutions were receiving a thorough going-over by critics of one kind or another, state legislatures went relatively untouched. While activists were marching on Washington for civil rights reform, while they were picketing the White House for change in the Vietnam policies, while they were rampant on college campuses in search of educational reform, nobody confronted Hartford, Albany, Tallahassee or Carson City demanding better state government.

Thus, virtually free from citizen pressure, the state legislatures have been easily approachable by special economic interests—insurance, oil, banking, building contractors, utilities, drug companies. Only recently, for example, Governor Marvin Mandel of Maryland held an all-day hearing to determine which bills passed by the legislature the public felt he should veto. Almost all of the seventy-five speakers heard represented one special interest group or another.

What *has* changed state legislatures more than anything else during the past few years has not been citizen pressure, but mandatory reapportionment. This has permitted stronger and more equitable representation for expanding urban and suburban areas in legislatures which were once dominated by rural-oriented lawmakers somewhat insensitive to the growing problems of modern living.

Also, until recently there has been little literature which prescribed methods by which to modernize the legislatures and encourage public interest. Among the most noted items now in print are the reports commissioned by the Eagleton Institute of Rutgers University, and the 1971 book by the Citizens' Conference on State Legislatures called *The Sometimes Governments*. They point out weaknesses and strengths, and make solid recommendations for updating and improvement.

Calling itself "an independent group of Americans" who "fervently believe that the 50 state legislatures are the heart of the governmental system in the United States," the Citizens' Conference asserted that these bodies:

> ... are supposed to give us the advantages of local government (its proximity to the people and the problems) without its disadvantages (parochialism, short-sightedness). They are, on the other hand, supposed to give us the advantages of a central government (broad perspective and powers, large human and financial resources, a single focus) without its disadvantages (remoteness, inflexibility, arbitrariness).

There can be no question about the importance of state government. Our Founding Fathers spelled out the specific domains of the Executive, Legislative and Judicial branches of the federal government and delegated all other powers to the states. These powers cover a diverse and continually growing spectrum from preservation of our ecological resources to preservation of human life. What better reasons for seeking a responsive and constructive state legislature through a forceful and persistent citizen presence?

This book, then, is less about the ills of Connecticut's or any other state's legislature than it is about how citizens in one state established an effective organization to cure or at least reduce its deficiencies. The story of our "General Assembly Project" can serve as a manual for people anywhere who want to monitor the behavior of elected officials and, where necessary, to change it. School boards, town and city councils, boards of tax review as well as legislatures could all benefit from the kind of attention that will be described in the following pages.

The Connecticut Citizen Action Group model is not perfect, but it is the first and only model of its kind. When the group was created in 1971 by Ralph Nader, it was designed to carry out pioneering projects of this type and to help people in other parts of the country borrow the best of the ideas and techniques that result from CCAG's experiences.

Feeling Our Way in the Dark

FOR SOME TIME before we approached the General Assembly Project, CCAG had been active as a group in the areas of consumer and human rights and environmental protection. Raising money under the ecology banner had made sense. Suburbanites and rural people, rather than the urban workers standing at downtown bus stops or leaving the factories at night, were the best potential contributors. Our April 1971, fund-raising campaign had been organized around Earth Week. Rallies, earth marches, bake and button sales, cocktail parties and "Pennies for Earth" projects by junior high school students had raised more than fifty thousand dollars to launch the Connecticut Earth Action Group (CEAG)—pronounced "siege."

Perhaps if we had stuck to the ecology issues, the funding problems we have had since would not have developed. More than a few nasty letters were received when we decided to change our name from "Earth Action" to "Citizen Action." But the character of citizen organizations is determined more by the personalities within them than anything else.

When our group was established by Ralph Nader, there were just four of us: Denny Chapman, a former VISTA volunteer, native of Connecticut and one of the creators of the National VISTA Alliance which was aimed at pressuring the Administration for greater support; Marty Rogol, a former VISTA lawyer in Cleveland, who earlier had left a prestigious Washington, D.C. law firm; Angie Martin, who worked with VISTA in Nevada; and myself, who had once joined the Department of Health, Education and Welfare in Washington as a liaison to street gangs. Later, while working for Senator Walter Mondale of Minnesota, I accepted Nader's offer to return to Connecticut and head the nation's first full-time public interest group on these issues.

Once our staff was put together, it became obvious that the "Earth Action" label would not do. We had come from varied backgrounds; from the federal bureaucracy, from law firms, from poverty programs. Although young, we were not the former leaders of the student, anti-war or educational reform movements. Our sympathies and sometimes our time had been loaned to these efforts, but we were not in the forefront of them.

Each of us in our own way had experienced frustration with parochial issues. The ex-VISTA members who had worked in central cities had often come up against a strong tide of opposition from people to whom they had no bridge. The "rednecks" didn't like poverty programs, but how could you do anything about changing the rednecks? Lawyers from Washington's best firms had been "guns for hire," often representing clients they knew they should be opposing. Theirs had been a closed world of long, martini-filled lunches and conversations with people who all sounded the same. While at HEW and later, I had dealt with educational reform, but usually from a distance, via student leaders and the educational establishment.

For all of us who had been in Washington, having the chance to work with people in local communities was a welcome challenge. The fantasy land of "national overviews,"of being "where the action is," could give you a tremendous illusion of self-importance while separating you from "the public" for whom you were supposedly working.

So "Earth Action" would not do. We all had had enough of being trapped in single issues, of being easily labeled. What we sought was an organizational framework that could not be put into one bag or another.

Though we worried about our newness in Connecticut, in a short time it was clear that we could overcome it on most issues. For example, in November 1971, with affidavits from workers on a weapons testing range, we burst on the national as well as the state scene with allegations that executives of Colt Firearms Company had ordered cheating in testing their M-16 rifle. Talk about issues with a broad base! When our charges were confirmed, both the conservative Veterans of Foreign Wars and the liberal Vietnam Veterans against the War applauded. This was an issue on which we had no opponents except the company management seeking to save its own skin and the Pentagon siding with its defense contractors.

Soon we were before the Public Utilities Commission fighting a phone company rate increase. Our intervention pierced what until that time had been a friendly, cordial atmosphere in which the utility companies asked for more than they needed, the PUC went through the motions of giving them a token slap on the wrist—and then approved sizable increases. Expecting to lose, we lost. But we were back again when the electric companies tried for what seemed almost a yearly increase. Just to make that milk-toast Commission come to life was worth the effort. Our expert

testimony and cross-examination of company witnesses de-
molished the club-like atmosphere of the hearing room.

In those first months of our existence we led massive
organizing moves to pack hearings on the state's air pollution
control plan. When an automobile dealer refused to discuss
with us what we felt was a valid complaint of a consumer
who had come to us in desperation, we enlisted a large
crowd to hand out lemons in front of his showroom. In less
than half an hour, he was willing to talk.

Indeed, we quickly developed an ability to reel in many
mini-victories. In the beginning we had made lists of projects
we thought might be worth doing: by our fifth month there
was no need to look for work. "It must be like the first
guy who ever fished off Newfoundland," a friend remarked.

Newness was not a problem when we were simply digging
for facts and offering our conclusions to the public. But
dealing with the legislature was another matter. Gaining
a reputation with the members for producing solid, factual
information was important in helping to pass good legislation. But when the same legislators had a choice of information from a new citizen group or "facts" offered by an
industry representative they had known for several years,
we wound up second best. The industry people had been
taking legislators to lunch and throwing parties for them
for decades. Almost all of the information available on bills
at the Capitol came from industry lobbyists. The situation
was alleviated somewhat by the addition of more full-time
legislative staffers, but the part-time Senators and Representatives, anxious for background data on a proposed bill,
more often than not continued to accept industry statements.

Many factors at the Capitol put citizen lobbyists at a
disadvantage. Our few lobbyists there were dealing with
a large number of legislators: 177 members of the House
and 36 of the Senate. Our group's first session at the Capitol,

in 1972, was also the first "annual session." Until that year Connecticut's legislature, like many others, had met only every second year. This had produced an almost complete dominance of state government by the Governor and his Executive Branch and had caused legislators to rely heavily on their party leaders. Indeed, the Governor and the few party leaders seemed at times to be the only players in the game, with the rank and file members simply going through the motions.

For their part-time work—which usually meant full-time for the more conscientious legislators—they had been receiving about four thousand dollars every two years. When in that 1972 session both houses voted themselves a sizable pay raise to six thousand dollars a year, the public screamed loud and long. A part of the opposition to the increase arose from the feeling that the legislators had been deceitful by not holding a public hearing on the issue.

The pay raise issue once again exposed the bad light in which the General Assembly was seen by the Connecticut public.Some of its indignation seemed justified to us in our first full session as lobbyists. We saw party leaders crumble before industry pressure on key consumer bills without so much as a word of disagreement from their rank and file members. We took part in public hearings which were "public" in name only. We found that key bills sometimes disappeared even though they had the support of many members. And we were shut out of secret committee meetings.

The legislative procedure was further debilitated and drained of credibility by the great number of bills introduced, nearly six thousand in 1971, of which only a small percentage were ever enacted into law. Many important bills would drop out of sight, to resurface only days before the end of the session. These weaknesses in the system led to widespread public disenchantment with and even ridicule of the General Assembly. Thus, as our efforts at the Capitol became visible to the public, we became a focal point for those who wanted to take part in improving the situation. The "Citizens'Lobby" which we created arose partially out of our becoming the focus for this citizen pressure, but also because, from the beginning, we had realized the importance of having concerned people feel a part of CCAG. Less than four months after we announced the lobby effort, we had organized more than three thousand people into a state-wide phone network to contact legislators and urge specific action.

In the field we were strong and getting stronger. But the other half of our lobbying effort, the day-in and day-out presence at the State Capitol, still suffered from our newness and inexperience. "Fred's been a respected member of the party for twenty-five years," said one Senator, referring to a powerful industry lobbyist. "When he asks, 'Will you go my way on this bill?' you tend to respect his word and go his way more than you would somebody you don't know that well." Like new citizen groups, presumably.

The professional lobbyists had the edge. That was no secret and no surprise, given the years of citizen neglect. But even with frustrations and setbacks, there were indications that we could make a difference, so we kept plugging away. With pressure in the districts, combined with lobbyists at the Capitol, the end of our first session found us chalking up some victories along with our defeats. The House Speaker said in a newspaper interview that he attributed the passage of two key environmental bills to CCAG, pointing out that in the previous year they had suffered resounding defeats. And our public criticism of the performance of a few legislative leaders appeared to have at least some impact on their subsequent behavior.

In the spring of 1972, toward the end of the legislative session, we began discussing how we might use the summer to expand our influence at the Capitol. At the same time, Ralph Nader's people in Washington were putting together an in-depth study of the U.S. Congress which was to highlight the record of each member. Borrowing ideas from Nader's Congress Project and combining them with some of our own, we prepared an outline for a possible Connecticut project. In early May, after talking with Ralph Nader and weighing the pros and cons among our permanent staff, we decided that the "General Assembly Project" would be "one" of our summer endeavors. Little did we realize at that time how much it would occupy, if not captivate, our lives for the next several months. There would, in fact, be no other summer projects. Nor would there be beach parties, fishing or any of those summer-fun diversions. We were setting off to take a long, hard look at our state legislature and by the time elections rolled around, it was to become the longest and hardest ever taken at a state legislature.

We approached the Project with excitement. With our first year of operation nearing completion, we had grown to love the organization and its work. No savior or martyr complexes spurred or plagued us. Long nights and dreary research were depressing at times, but we could still say we enjoyed what we were doing.

We had no illusions. With the experiences gained in VISTA, law firms, HEW, political campaigns and other frustrating existences, we knew better than to expect dramatic, instant changes. What we had learned and come to expect during that year, however, was that our fast-improving ability to size up issues, develop a strategy and then do the hard work would eventually lead to important, if not earth-shattering, changes.

Holding Fast, Hanging Loose

WHAT PUT US in this position? And what do our experiences mean for other groups who are considering projects similar to this?

There were many factors involved, but most of all, we had the troops. While I don't want to give the impression that we had great legions of citizen volunteers, we did have many, among them lawyers, people with scientific backgrounds and community organizers, who had been working full-time for more than a year on other projects for CCAG.

The time demanded of our staff and the pressure exerted on them because of the nature of our work was great. But because of their backgrounds, this was not a new experience—a factor not to be underestimated! Spending long hours at the office was not a novelty; meeting deadlines was familiar. You could find people at our office any time but Sunday mornings. And most staff members did not leave until ten or eleven at night.

In addition, our people were not easily intimidated by having to deal with lawmakers. Of course, there were some in our Citizens' Lobby who felt timid and tentative, awed at the beginning by prestigious titles, but we watched them gain confidence as they became more involved with legislative issues. Those first few calls were difficult and certainly some people were intimidated by legislators who told them, "You have a nerve calling me," or "You don't know what you're talking about." But most of the citizen lobbyists had found that by reading our mailings on proposed bills they were sufficiently informed to gain the respect of legislators. In some instances, Senators or Representatives even called our lobbyists asking for more information on a particular bill. There's nothing like having a legislator ask for help to make you more confident.

More important than the confidence gained by the lobbyists in the field, however, was the attitude of the full-time staff members. Our prior experience was crucial to the General Assembly Project's success. Marty Rogol calls it "a political sense," and feels that no citizen group should undertake a project of this type, even scaled down to the local level, unless it has within it some staffers who are accustomed to dealing with public officials—people who can be tough without being rude and persistent without being unreasonable.

We were fortunate to have such people—former government employees, an aide to a U.S. Senator, Legal Aid lawyers and former VISTA volunteers—all accustomed to dealing with power structures.

We were certainly given every opportunity to wilt or withdraw from the plans that had been drawn up on paper—when the announcement of those plans met with hostile reaction from some legislators and mass media members; when representatives of more traditional groups backed off from cooperation in such a "controversial" undertaking; and, mostly, when we became fully aware of the volume of information needed to complete the profiles.

Flexibility was another key reason the General Assembly Project was possible. So many citizen groups become paralyzed, hung up on their own structures, rules and procedures. Boards of directors and bureaucratic hierarchies lead to slow decision making and boring meetings, which in turn cause unnecessary and costly delays and bring momentum to a crashing halt. I recall with great pain the number of times during the legislative session preceding our study when we sought to enlist community groups in support or opposition of key pieces of legislation. Many individuals who said they agreed with us and would like to help also said they could not make decisions without consulting their boards—which met on the third Thursday of every month.

By the need for flexibility and quick response I don't mean to suggest that you should sacrifice control and accountability. I realize that the reason for having boards of directors and fixed procedures is to provide proper checks on the conduct of staff members, insure consistency in the groups' positions and maintain an orderly turnover of leadership. But our experience has been that too often these legitimate needs are overemphasized at the expense of getting things done. (This is also true, by the way, of nonpartisanship. For fear of appearing one-sided, too many groups tend toward inertia.)

Speed and flexibility were crucial in this Project as they are with most projects we do. We had to decide on courses of action quickly; we had to react quickly and be able to make small changes in our procedures to suit the needs of our staff and facilitate the Project's completion. Yes, we had a Board of Directors which included three lawyers who worked with Ralph.All three took an active interest in our work, but none of them demanded to be consulted before every decision was made.

To be sure, Ralph wanted to be consulted and kept informed on major matters. I had been in touch with him almost daily while the Citizens'Lobby was investigating the possibility of cheating on the testing of the M-16 rifle at Colt Firearms in Hartford. When the Navy spilled radioactive wastewater into the Thames River near New London, Nader and our organization jointly criticized its failure to produce an environmental impact statement on the waste disposal process it was using. And we had talked to Ralph at length about the General Assembly Project itself, mostly to obtain ideas on the best way to proceed. But we were never told to consult him or other board members before making our next move.

The decision-making process at CCAG might best be described as collective in the beginning, but ultimately unilateral. While Bill Sklar, a University of Connecticut law student, had been investigating the M-16 cheating charges, for example, he worked largely on his own, but checked with me frequently for advice on how we should proceed. Or when our consumer attorney, Marty Rogol, was representing us in the electricity rate case before the Public Utilities Commission, he and I formulated a general strategy for the group and he developed his own plan within that framework. For Angie Martin, who coordinates the Citizens' Lobby, finding good people and keeping them informed of the legislative issues is her own thing.

But we never really sacrificed control. Final decisions were made by me as Director, and all statements to the press were decided on beforehand, more or less collectively, and then usually delivered by Marty, Angie or me.

The organization that evolved from this type of planning became ideally suited to gathering information for preparation of legislative profiles. The staffers who had been with us for a year or more were accustomed to our system, and

I do not believe that the new workers who joined us were intimidated by it. There may have been some resentment initially because a few people felt they were excluded from decision making about the general direction the Project was to take, but we had no real problems in that regard.

In other projects, our uniformity and control had helped us achieve some pretty fair results and, perhaps more importantly, improved our reputation with the media. We had good relations with the press in general, especially for a group not operating with funds or authority bestowed by either the state or the corporate world. (Such are often written off by the media as "non-legitimate.") We had partly surmounted that potential problem by building a record as a group that delivered the goods as promised.

For example, the press was aware that our accusations about the M-16 had been upheld and the practices in question halted. It was also aware that we had brought charges against Governor Meskill for appointing individuals to a power-siting council, who had friends in the utility that council would regulate, as well as the fact that these accusations had been later substantiated. The press knew, too, that we had accused the Citizens' Committee to Keep Connecticut Clean and Beautiful of being a waste of money, a body filled with representatives of the corporations which had helped create the state's litter problem—the bottle and can manufacturers and sellers. And the press knew that the Council had later been abolished.

So we were no strangers to the press. But just as important was the fact that our media coverage did not result solely from our accomplishments on the issues. It never should. You need people with a knowledge of the different media, how they work and how they can be used to your group's advantage. You should know, for example, the individuals in management, editorial and reporting positions. You must determine who is most likely to support you on each particular issue. There are editors in Connecticut, as there no doubt are in any state, who think our stand in opposition to construction of certain highways is counterproductive, but they admire our work on automobile complaints. I know one editor who says he can't get excited about environmental issues but is wild about our work on food additives!

Beyond personalities, you have to learn how these media work. Which papers have evening editions and which have morning? How many of each are there in your region or state? Which papers reach the most people? Which are most sympathetic to your positions and projects? What is the best way to get your story on radio? Which stations are anxious to accept those forty-second statements about your project? Which stations have talk shows that will interview your speakers? After you know these answers, you can decide when and where to release reports, statements or whatever. This can be a very complex game.

It is very important to have a group project represented publicly by a minimum number of speakers so that it will be identified in the minds of the press and the public with specific personalities, thus creating a minimum of confusion and "humanizing" it.

I will talk more about these questions later, but the point to be made here is that CCAG had invaluable answers to most of them through prior experience, on-the-job learning, common sense and, sometimes, just plain luck.

We tried never to become embroiled in staff in-fighting and introspection or allow the focus of the organization to be shifted from crises on the outside to self-imposed catastrophes on the inside. Perhaps the best way to convey the atmosphere which characterized the Project office was a willingness to give and accept criticism and suggestions. Increasingly however, our researchers found that although they had flexibility in examining the legislators for which they were responsible, it was extremely important to maintain a uniform approach and framework for maximum results and impact on both the legislature and the public.

Although we had been involved in many issues during the preceding year, we never could have carried out this particular Project without the help of other groups. We especially needed them to tell us which pieces of legislation had been important to them during the past session and which bills they would be pushing in the coming year. We then planned to include their names on our interview forms so that we could place legislators on record as being for or against them.

One of the greatest obstacles to working with other groups—even greater than their potential inability to react quickly—is the petty in-fighting often found within and among them. Most of this stems from a desire to get the credit. We were no different from any other group in wanting attribution for our work; solid citizen groups are not built, after all, on complete selflessness. But we discovered an interesting tactic, a barter system in a way: we were at times willing to trade our credit for their cooperation—subtly, but effectively.

Because we were a full-time group with flexibility and ample office space just a four-minute walk from the State Capitol, we could offer assistance to the part-time, more traditional groups that existed outside of Hartford or the groups that had perhaps only one employee. In fact, this was one of the key factors of the concept that CCAG was created to represent.

So we told groups which asked us for information that the end result of the Project, its legislative profiles, would enable them to pinpoint positions of legislators in their area of interest. Women's rights advocates, for example, wanted us to ask the legislators for their views on the Equal Rights Amendment, pregnancy leave and abortion. Labor groups welcomed the opportunity to find out where legislators stood on unemployment compensation for strikers as well as a general picture of how they viewed organized labor.

The responses to such questions would later become invaluable not only to these and other groups such as environmentalists, mass transportation advocates and consumer organizations, but also to corporations and their executive committees.

Applying Ideas and Techniques

SPEAKING BEFORE the National Press Club on November 2, 1971, Ralph Nader announced his plans to finance and lead "what is probably the most comprehensive and detailed study of the (U.S.) Congress since its establishment."

He outlined how the Congress Project mainly would be carried out by about eighty graduate students and young professionals conducting research in Washington, D.C. over a period of a year. "It [the study] will range from an analysis of the electoral and campaign process to individual profiles of members of Congress to the internal workings of the legislature and its interactions with the Executive Branch and private constituencies."

By June of 1972 the Congress Project had gained definite direction and shape and considerably more workers than at first anticipated. A description of the massive effort published in that month stated:

The Project includes extensive surveys of mayors, governors, state legislators, former members of Congress, press, interest group advocates, academicians, local party officials, former opponents, legislative representatives and aides of members, several thousand ex-local community leaders and all the Members themselves. Non-partisan volunteer researchers of all ages have been recruited in every State Capitol and in the districts of almost every Member of Congress.

Although the CCAG had been in operation for only a couple of months when the Congress Project was announced, I spoke to Ralph almost immediately, asking him if he thought the same kind of approach could be used to scrutinize a state legislature. To "focus citizen attention upon the Congress" was a constantly advertised goal of the Nader Congress Project. What institutions, including the Congress, are more ignored and more in need of citizen attention than the state legislatures?

Ralph said he thought it could and should be done in Connecticut, and during the organizing and fund-raising efforts in Connecticut in the spring of 1972, Nader and others often said that applying the ideas and techniques in state capitols that he had used in Washington could produce results. All of us involved in creating CCAG, both in Connecticut and Washington, felt that the partnership between the national and state projects would be beneficial to both.

It was, of course, the tremendous difference between the U.S. Congress and the state legislatures that was to impose a limit on what elements of the Congress Project were applicable to Connecticut's General Assembly. As in most state legislatures, its members serve part-time, are severely lacking in staff and facilities, and generally do not enjoy the visibility, the information-gathering mechanisms or the expertise of the federal body's members. The Congress Project itself was also much more academically oriented than we either wanted or had the capacity to be in Connecticut.

A six-page detailed outline, supposedly the basis for the subsequently published book, *Who Runs Congress?*, included, among other things, sections on "The American Vision of Congress," "Representative Democracy," "Power and Democracy in Congress" and "Power of the Purse."

In one of his many meetings with our staff during the year, Ralph suggested that our Project should be much less scholarly than his Washington effort. Not that he was advising us to put less emphasis on research; we simply needed to concentrate more on the specific records of legislators rather than on the institution itself. Because of tremendous limitations on staff, funds and the availability of records from which to analyze the lawmaking body, we had to place our emphasis where it would pack the most immediate wallop—namely in providing information to the electorate on what were usually specific but little-known records and views of their state representatives.

The Congress Project offered us much more than the idea and example for our Project, however. Some of its actual materials and approaches were applicable and practical for our Project and there is no doubt that we saved a great deal of time and gained considerable guidance from the opportunity to be in close contact with the Washington people.

In early May they mailed the first large packet of material to us. It included an outline of the Congress Project, instructions for field researchers in each Congressional district in the country, and lengthy questionnaires for various individuals in districts where interviews were to be sought. Among the people to be contacted in each member's district were:

—the district office head;
—the leader of the member's party in the district;
—the leader of the opposition party in the district;

—mayors, city managers and selectmen;
—the member's opponent in the last election;
—and a host of "community leaders."

We made best use of this last questionnaire both because we were short on time and people and because interviewing political and elected leaders in a state legislator's district would more probably yield information tainted with the "party line" than substantive facts on the legislator's performance. And we felt that a number of opinions from within each member's district on his performance would provide additional insight for constituents.

The list of community leaders the Congress Project suggested should be contacted from any one district included:

—the head of the district's largest bank;
—the president of the company with the most employees;
—the head of the Chamber of Commerce in the largest city;
—the head of the Labor Council or largest labor union;
—the head of the largest farmers' organization (if applicable);
—the leader of the Council of Churches or a similar organization;
—leaders of minority groups;
—the head of the largest chapter of the League of Women Voters; and
—leaders of at least two of the largest citizen groups.

In addition to adopting the community leaders' questionnaire, we found the Congress Project's instructions for surveying local newspapers very helpful. The basic goal of the Nader newspaper survey was to determine how much coverage was given to a particular member of Congress by the largest newspaper in his district. Major articles about the member from the previous two years were sought. Among the questions to be answered by the researchers were:

—Who owns the newspaper?
—Does the member have any financial connection with the paper?
—Does the newspaper keep a clipping file about the member?
—What is the general policy on permitting public inspection of the files?
—Are copies or microfilms of back issues available?
—Are you allowed to view them?
—Is there an index to back issues?

Finally, the newspaper survey form asked these questions about each newspaper's coverage of the member:

—Describe any slogans used in the member's campaign.
—Did the newspaper endorse the member?
—Does the member have a regular column in the paper?
—Does the paper carry a regular report of the member's voting record?
—What is the name of the local political reporter for the paper?

But even more helpful than what we received from the community leaders and newspaper survey forms was the information in the questionnaire for the members themselves. From that massive document—it contained more than six hundred questions—we selected the basis for the outline of our own Project. So by mid-May we had decided to focus on the following aspects of each legislator's record:

—Voting records on key consumer, environmental and human rights issues.

—Absentee records.

—Statements made on the issues in floor debates, public hearings, town meetings, newsletters, newspaper articles and columns, radio and TV programs, speeches, lectures and other public appearances.

—Service to constituents, including ways in which member keeps constituents informed about the issues, ways in which member learns about constituent views, and new forums for citizen participation which member promotes.

—Preparedness on issues, seeking to determine how well prepared member has been on important issues and how his/her knowledge about them is acquired.

—Campaign sources of contributions; promises; affiliations of contributors and campaign staff; donations of services and materials to campaign; endorsements received and endorsements given during the campaign.

—Economic and occupational background and what aspects of them may have presented conflicts of interest on legislation or other legislative business.

—Profiles of leadership for members holding such positions with party or committee, and how they have used or abused these positions.

It would be impossible to speculate on how the CCAG could have gone about the General Assembly Project without the Congress Project's direction. But even with such guidance, we floundered at some points, erred at others, and at the beginning had only a general idea of the torturous work that lay ahead.

Getting The Word Out

IT STANDS TO REASON that if you pay people very little, you can afford to hire more people. If a citizen group pays an attorney twenty thousand dollars and a secretary ten thousand dollars, it won't get all that much for its money. But if you hire two lawyers, a scientist and a community organizer for five thousand dollars each, your expenses are going to be something else again. That's what we did. We had been lucky to find people who were not only qualified but deeply committed to our work, and they had become our paid full-time staff.

We now frantically began to look for volunteers to work full-time for this particular Project. Confronted with the prospect of preparing in-depth profiles of up to two hundred legislators by fall, we needed at least ten to fifteen people.

Finding them was not easy. You hear a great deal about volunteerism, and in fact you frequently hear people say that they would welcome an opportunity to become involved, but let's face it, there are simply not that many people you can count on in a pinch, especially when you're asking them to give up an entire summer.

We had become fairly adept at weeding out the good workers from the bad, the live ones from the deadwood, those who persevered from the fast-start-early-fade bunch. Even so, our rate of retaining volunteers had not been exactly super that first year, probably because we did not feel it worthwhile to do the "hand-holding" some people seemed to require. We tried to give people an early orientation on what their responsibilities would be and then ask them to undertake their jobs without bugging a lot of staff members along the way.

We were finally able to attract five additional people for our full-time Project staff. Some asked for absolutely no money. Others said that if we provided lodging, they would ask for twenty dollars per week for food. Nobody who came in especially for the Project received over twenty-five dollars per week.

The new staff members were college students, people between jobs, former state employees, social workers, school teachers off for the summer and housewives. They had been attracted to us in different ways and for different reasons. John Wancheck, for example, was about to enter his last semester at the University of Connecticut:

> I wound up with what was going to be a free summer and was trying to line up something that would be beneficial to what my line of interest was. I wasn't interested in making money. I deliberately went to the library looking for something coming out of this group. When I saw the newsletter, I found that there was this legislative study which, being in political science and being interested in law, I just picked right up ... They just said come in ... and asked me to come back for the organizing meeting that night.

Alexandra Woods, a junior at Smith College, learned

about CCAG from Debbie Gottheil, a housemate of hers who was working part-time for CCAG:

> I decided last fall, I guess early on, that I wanted to work in the states. I had had jobs in London in past summers. So I ruminated around and made applications with regional planning agencies and community groups in the Northampton area. ... I didn't know Debbie very well, but she was in the same house as I and I overheard what she was doing at CCAG. Debbie asked did I want this job, it might be open. She did say too, that you were trying to get only Connecticut people, so it was really off and on. And then, at the last moment, Debbie said it would be okay if I came down.

Debbie Gottheil had been with us a year before as a sophomore at Smith College, working on energy problems, especially nuclear safety issues. Her work-study arrangement with Smith gradually evolved into spending almost all of her time with us and in May she switched to the General Assembly Project. Portia Iverson had heard me speak at Colby College. She contacted me in early summer and came to work for us for twenty dollars per week. Emily Thomson had worked with us on weekends and vacations while home from Wheaton College in Massachusetts. Upon graduation in May, she arrived at CCAG to offer her services for the summer. And Nancy Carroll, a school teacher from Windsor, had helped us on a variety of projects, including the organization of the Citizens' Lobby in her area.

With these active, energetic people, we now had a nucleus from which to direct our volunteer search.

We tried as much as possible to rely on Connecticut residents, but Alexandra seemed too good to pass up and Debbie, though from Long Island, had worked with us long enough to have shed her carpetbagger image. I felt strongly about the need for Connecticut people because I knew we might be criticized for importing out-of-staters to investigate the records of Connecticut legislators. Having worked with Allard Lowenstein's Congressional campaign on Long Island in 1970, I had seen the disadvantages of having busloads of students from schools like Notre Dame and Michigan flood the district when local people were suspicious about the campaign from the beginning.

There was a great deal of work to be done, but none of us came close to realizing the enormity of it. If we had, a more elaborate recruiting system would have been set up. After all, a project of this type relies most heavily for its success not on planning or facilities or money but on the caliber of the people involved.

A full-time volunteer recruiter would have been most helpful. As it was we tried to get the word out about the planned Project and then talk to anyone who indicated an interest in helping. Some things we did right in recruiting; others we didn't.

First of all, the people who are most likely to be interested are young people. Most of us realize now that there is nothing special about the young in terms of their abilities or even in terms of extra willingness to work for change. And more and more of us involved in community organizing understand better now the need to involve people of all ages in our work, for to be labeled a youth group can be the kiss of death to effectiveness and appeal.

But the fact is that young people usually have more spare time than any other age group. They have more energy and they can, in many cases, afford to work for little or no money. The absence of four kids and a mortgage also means that—if they are perceptive enough to do it—they can afford to take more risks than the average person. And though many young people are understandably lacking in community work, and some have real difficulty in working outside the walls of the campus, they are also more likely than many other people to have recent research experience.

In some cases, and this is increasingly true, students may be able to receive academic credit for their work with an organization in the community. (There are, of course, different opinions as to whether credit should be given for this kind of work. My own view is that the extension of credit is overdone and that too frequently students take on projects simply because they will receive credit for them.) But in our case, working on an in-depth evaluation of the performances of state legislators was more likely to be a "meaningful learning experience," as educators like to call it, than anything that took place in a course on state government within the confines of a classroom.

Most organizations that would undertake this kind of project would not be on campus. (At least I hope they wouldn't: community-based groups are much more natural initiators.) But you need campus help. In a few cases, we went to professors and graduate students in political science, economics, sociology and other social science fields and asked them to help us recruit volunteers for the summer effort. In many academic institutions, professors can now suggest and approve independent study projects for their students. If possible, we found it is not a bad idea to attempt to recruit the professors themselves, at least as once-in-a-while consultants to your project. The contacts you make, of course, may also be of great assistance when you address your next issue.

If a project of this kind is planned far enough in advance, it is also a good idea to stop in on the financial aid people. Work-study programs often allow students to receive pay for working in a community project and most students find this preferable to the library or cafeteria. Given the current dearth of summer jobs, you may find that even students who have had work-study grants approved are nonetheless looking for employment. Usually the employer has to pay twenty per cent of the salary while the institution contributes the rest. Which usually means that for twenty dollars a week or less you can have a full-time worker on your staff. Campus newspapers and bulletin boards should help attract work-study people.

As I mentioned, good fortune more than good planning enabled us to initially attract an excellent core staff for the legislative work. In that process we learned a number of things about attracting people for projects like this, the first of which was that not many people want to give up an entire summer to research state legislators' records. And if a summer is going to be given up, most people do not want to do it for free. Many young people work on construction jobs, at drive-in restaurants or on other routine, summer occupations, dreading every day but making a considerable amount of money for next year's tuition.

There are also people who will convince themselves that they want to give up their summer but then will fade along the way. The extent of the drudgery of dull research is as difficult to anticipate as the thrills of completing a project like this. So the eighty-hour weeks can begin to take their toll in the form of turnover, which we could not afford. We simply could not have a person research the records of a number of legislators, become more and more familiar with the details of those records—and then leave the material for someone else to compile. We had this happen in a very few instances and the quality of the final written profiles on those legislators was not as outstanding as when the same person did the preliminary research, the community interviews and then the interview with the legislator.

Turnover is unfair to the legislator as well. To ensure

that a legislator would provide frank answers to questions and then continue to cooperate even when he was becoming increasingly nervous about the Project—or even hostile—required that one person deal with him for the Project's duration. As Alexandra Woods said, "It was probably my own naivete that made it happen, but I feel that it took me quite a while to reach the point where these people would trust me enough to cooperate with us."

There were numerous cases where our workers had to persist for weeks in order to pin down legislators on dates for interviews. In those instances as well, it was important that the legislator obtain the impression that this one person would not go away until an interview was held.

For the person who could not spend eighty hours a week studying state legislators but who sincerely wanted to help in some way, we developed limited involvement roles such as clipping public statements by area legislators or articles about them from their local newspapers. We also asked local volunteers to suggest names of community leaders and other constituents with an interest in state legislation so that we might interview them when we reached that portion of the Project.

An important point about organizing volunteers, we felt, was to develop roles whereby they could become involved in their own way, on their own time. People seem to be exhibiting more and more anti-organization or anti-joining tendencies and it is possible to lose some good workers by insisting that they join, join, join or commit themselves to an all-or-nothing involvement.

We also had handled our original Citizens' Lobby in this manner. Although we had wanted to mobilize as many people as possible to lobby for social legislation, we decided against setting up a structure with regular meeting nights and committee assignments. Instead, we told people that the Citizens' Lobby was designed for those who might not be especially crazy about joining yet another organization and becoming obligated to attend yet more dreary meetings. (Suburban communities, in particular, are glutted with such organizations, many of which do worthwhile work but require a commitment people are unwilling to make.)

We told them that they need not lobby for every bill, but that we would appreciate their passing on information about all the bills through the phone network we had established across the state. They could do all this from home: no babysitters, no week-night meetings, no annual banquets or balls.

Those who were most excited about the idea usually became regional coordinators, of which we had a total of twenty-seven. Each of them recruited twenty-five people in their own region to make phone calls, write letters and, in rare instances, visit their legislators. Those twenty-five people recruited five more. (In order to avoid toll calls, which is one of the fastest ways to curtail citizen action, each region was limited to local call areas.) Thus we were provided with "regulars" and a flexibility to recruit the others we so badly needed.

Recruiting through the media, especially radio, was a valuable tool for us, particularly on the General Assembly Project. Public Service Announcements (PSAs) are, according to Federal Communications Commission regulations, open to community groups. Each radio or TV station has a public affairs director and it is not a bad idea to meet with him, particularly if your project is "controversial" in the community. We found it important to let these media people know that we were not far-out fanatics.

We simply typed out our PSAs on a clean sheet of paper and sent copies to all the radio and TV stations. We all knew what the typical PSA sounded like:

The East River Lions Club will conduct its annual clambake at Shady Grove on Sunday, August 23, from 10 AM to sundown. For more information, contact. . . .

This kind of canned approach should be avoided. As long as you have free time to get your message across, make the most of it. A couple of years earlier, if we had been doing the General Assembly Project, we probably would have written our PSA this way:

The Connecticut Citizen Action Group (CCAG) is conducting an evaluation of the performances of state legislators. Volunteers are needed for research and interviewing.
For more information, contact. . . .

But experience has shown that viewing your PSA as a production and using some imagination helps immensely. Here's what one of our PSAs on the General Assembly Project said:

Are you out of school this summer—and out of a job? There's a very old institution that could stand some looking into. It's called the General Assembly. Why not help the Connecticut Citizen Action Group take a hard look at what legislators have been doing for the past two years. You won't make much money, but the rewards are many. Please contact CCAG at. . . .

Other PSAs should be focused toward housewives, retired people, teachers off for the summer and so forth. For students we found both AM and FM rock stations important. And campus radio stations shouldn't be forgotten. We have learned that they may even want to become partners and promoters in the recruiting drive. While you certainly don't want to look like a campus project, you have to be perceptive enough to take advantage of the desire by certain elements on the campus to touch, feel and affect the world outside the campus walls.

PSAs should be viewed, by the way, much the same as letters to the editor—without any illusions about their effectiveness. They may not bring crowds to your door but there is no doubt that they are good publicity for your group. They let people know that you are in existence and that you are working on important issues. All this has a cumulative effect and may be extremely important when it comes time not only to recruit people, but to attract financial support as well.

Talk-show hosts should be approached, directly if possible. Because our group had been visible and active before, we already were familiar with many around the state. These programs are interested in something new, so play up the unique features of what you are doing. We billed our Project (accurately) as "the first project of its kind in the nation, the most in-depth analysis of a state legislature ever performed by citizens." And it is important to choose your speaker for these appearances carefully. If he or she is abrasive, dull, cocky or withdrawn, it can really hurt.

Inexpensive but eye-catching posters and leaflets placed on bulletin boards in supermarkets, schools, churches and elsewhere can, like the PSAs, not only help recruit but are good advertisements for the group.

From the beginning, our media coverage of the Project was short of spectacular. The only reason we received modest initial coverage was that we played up the "conflicts" angle. The launching of a study of the state legislature by a citizens' organization is hardly major news. But an "investigation" of "conflicts of interest" is something else.

So on May 16, 1972, the *Hartford Courant* ran a story on our announced Project headlined: "Interest Conflict Probe Opens. Legislators Under Scrutiny." The Fairfield County weekly, *Fairpress*, wrote, "Probe Of Lawmakers Planned."

The New York Times was most accurate in describing what we were intending to do. "Connecticut Group to Compare Legislators' Pledges and Records, " its May 21 article began, and then continued:

> When Connecticut's 213 legislators return home from the current special session of the General Assembly, they will all find themselves under investigation.
>
> Their voting records on environmental, consumer and human rights bills in the last few years will be scrutinized. Their speeches and promises made during public hearings, closed legislative committee meetings, radio and television shows, and election campaigns will be viewed. Their professional clients will be disclosed in any possible cases of conflict of interests.

An Associated Press story in the May 17 *Bridgeport Telegram* dwelt on financial disclosure. It opened with, "Some Legislators are Angered by 'Citizens' Lobby' Questionnaire," and stated:

> An investigation of state legislators by a "citizens' lobby" affiliated with Ralph Nader is going to encounter considerable resistance from the lawmakers, judging by a sampling of opinion at the State Capitol Tuesday.
>
> Some legislators presented with a copy of the Connecticut Citizens' Action Group's questionnaires exploded into unprintable comments. "They must be crazy to think I'd fill this out," said one legislator.

There were a few editorials on the announcement of our Project. One in the *New Haven Register* highlighted both our Project and a national Ford Foundation effort to reform state legislatures. Again, the conflicts aspect of our Project, only a minor portion of the entire effort, was singled out and expanded:

> Last week ... an announcement was made in Hartford by the Connecticut Citizen Action Group, a Ralph Nader organization, of the initiation of a probing look at the conflict of interests problem as it exists in our General Assembly. ...
>
> The Nader group has taken a more specific approach [from the Ford Foundation], as is the way of the nation's number one consumer advocate, and is addressing itself to a problem that has lain just below the surface of legislative activity for some time. The group hopes to have the results of its study available before the November election. ...
>
> It will be interesting to see which of the legislative reform efforts, the Nader study or the Ford Foundation program, produces the desired results.

By June, most of the news on the Project was in local papers, especially weeklies which were beginning to highlight the responses of area legislators to our preliminary questionnaire. Under the headline "Local Legislators Object To CCAG Questionnaire," one wrote:

> The Connecticut Citizen Action Group won't be receiving many questionnaires from Fairfield County legislators, if a brief survey of local representatives is any indication.

We were to find, however, that by July when we made our phone calls to the lawmakers with requests for interviews, personal contacts had changed the image of the

Project in the minds of many of them. And the large number of those agreeing to interviews confirmed our hunch.

"Legislators Okay Personal Quiz," read a headline in the *Waterbury Republican* on July 21, 1972. It followed with:

> Connecticut legislators who balk at filling out questionnaires that ask pointed questions about finances readily agree to personal interviews, reports a citizens group investigating legislators.
>
> Only 12 of the 213 members of the General Assembly have refused any cooperation so far with the Connecticut Citizen Action Group, said CCAG director, Toby Moffett. [*The number later grew to 18.*]

With the exception of the TV coverage of our training session for interviewers in late July, there would be no more media coverage of the Project until near its completion, when we managed to drum up some advance stories on the Project's release to the public.

Bearding the Lawmakers

OUR FIRST STEP in approaching the lawmakers was to send them a preliminary questionnaire (see Appendix for details) designed with three specific goals in mind: to gather basic, introductory information on the people with whom we would be dealing; to separate those who agreed to cooperate from those who hesitated and to prepare ourselves to cope with the latter; and to let the legislators know what the General Assembly Project was, the reasons for it and that we meant to be successful.

Substantial press coverage insured that most legislators would learn of the Project even without receiving letters and questionnaires from us. Most of those who were unhappy with our plans focused their dismay on the request for full disclosure of financial assets and liabilities as well as a statement asking for names of corporate clients, if any.

While some voiced little or no comment, possibly through indifference, approval or a wait-and-see attitude, others were extremely vocal, raising objections for which groups in other states might be prepared.

"I don't even tell my wife who my clients are," said the House Majority Leader. Having just turned forty, he admits to a somewhat different political persuasion than he espoused a decade earlier when he first ran for the General Assembly. "I've come full circle. I used to be one of the great civil libertarians because I could easily afford to be."

Later he wrote me:

> As an attorney, I never disclose the name of any client without his specific direction to do so—I fail to see what advantage is served by knowing my yearly income beyond pure curiosity. I do not believe that one seeking legislative office is required to bare his soul in relation to every facet of his personal and business life.

One Senator went directly to the press upon receiving our letter and, addressing CCAG through the *Vernon Enquirer,*he said, "My ... earnings, my net worth, assets, liabilities, holdings are frankly and bluntly none of your business."

Sometime later he called and insisted that we make an appointment to discuss the Project. He wanted to know, he said, which conflicts we had uncovered so far. "Tell me where the conflicts are and I'll help you expose them," he suggested, tongue-in-cheek. But by that time it had been announced that he would not be running for re-election, and we could not spend the time to interview him under those circumstances.

I must say that I did spend almost two hours on the phone with him that day and our intense discussion on conflicts of interest and financial disclosures came to an abrupt, albeit cordial, conclusion when he admitted the reason for his reluctance: "I don't want people to know how poor I am."

Although he may or may not have been joking, it was an interesting point. Most people feel that public officials who try to hide their income do so because they have large hidden assets or unsavory sources of income, but keeping up with the Joneses also plays a sizable part in refusals to disclose finances.

One Representative, a former college economics instructor whose constituency includes the University of Connecticut community, raised the point in a question and answer period following a speech to a conference of young trade unionists. Responding to a question from CCAG staffer Marty Rogol on the subject of the questionnaire, she said, "I do plan to return [it], and I probably will include the income of myself and my husband [a political science professor at the university], but I'm not sure it's fair to ask others."

"Like whom?"

"Well, for instance, we have some people in the General Assembly who are not wealthy. We have a bricklayer and a few people who work the night shift. It just might be embarrassing to them to have to reveal how little they make. What if a guy makes $7,500 a year?"

A young union member was out of his seat. "I make $7,500 a year and I wouldn't be ashamed to admit it," he said.

Others joined him in support and it was a fine though unexpected boost for the Project.

A freshman Representative (like her colleague just mentioned, one of the most well-informed and conscientious) responded with a letter:

> I think I know what you're trying to uncover with the preliminary questionnaire, though I'm not sure how productive this approach will be. I *am* sure you'll get your headlines and I'm also sure you will have ruffled lots of legislative feathers—in some cases quite unfairly.

She then answered all questions on our preliminary form except those relating to income. "You'll find that some questions have not been answered, frankly, because I don't think it's any of your business."

Some of the twenty women legislators also told us that their husbands would not allow them to reveal the family income to outsiders.

Among the other public statements or letters to CCAG by legislators who felt that the request for disclosure was an invasion of privacy, the one having the strongest, most publicized and greatest impact on our entire study came from the House Minority Leader, a six-year veteran of the General Assembly. He gave the *Hartford Courant* his political philosophy in a nutshell:

> Take females—as far as I'm concerned, some are good looking, the others are beautiful. I'm a liberal on some issues, a conservative on others, and practical on most.

On most, yes. But after receiving our initial letter, the soon-to-be Speaker of the House did something he apparently regretted later. In a letter to all members of his party he announced, "As a matter of information, you might be interested to know that I have disposed of my questionnaire in the wastebasket. . . ."

During his interview later he would refer to the episode as "that little thing we had earlier in the summer" and "an honest difference of opinion." Sitting across from him in his law office, I almost thanked him for doing it, for he provided visibility and credibility to our Project which we could not have achieved with a hundred press releases of our own.

With a substantial outpouring from legislators against our request for full financial disclosure and even some from the press, we began to lose a little of our confidence. Not much, but just enough to establish and set down why we believed legislators should make their money matters public.

Our discussions with Ralph Nader and people at the Congress Project had been somewhat helpful. Once we realized that we did not have to pretend that we represented the "public" as all things to all men, and that we did not have to assert that the citizenry was in *complete* agreement with our positions, we felt liberated. Finally we hammered out a position which was basically this:

> We are merely a group of citizens. We have a right to ask legislators for their financial backgrounds. They, in turn, have a perfect right to refuse. No law requires public disclosure. We, however, have a right to publicize their refusals. And the public has a right to draw conclusions based on the information we provide.

This policy statement was immensely helpful to us because so many legislators and other people—supporters and detractors alike—tried to nail us with the question, "How can you say you represent the public?"

Now that we had a general policy statement, we also realized the need for a specific position on and definition of a "conflict of interests." Help came from a review of previous literature on the subject; from a study of laws of other states (only Illinois requires full public disclosure of finances of its public officials); and from John Gardner's citizen group, *Common Cause*, which had drafted a model conflicts of interest law for states and sponsored a Colorado project revolving around the financial backgrounds of its state legislators.

Our position was basically a recognition that conflicts

of interest were inevitable in some form, particularly in a part-time legislature composed primarily of self-employed professionals. But, we said, there were both avoidable and unavoidable conflicts. The unavoidable resulted from the reality that most legislators were also professionals in fields that could create conflicts of interest on many bills. For instance, a lawyer could have a vested interest in safe boating laws or changes in the probate system. Realtors and insurance agents would find similar instances of conflicting interests.

The avoidable conflicts were much more obvious: realtors voting on bills concerning licensing of their profession, or grocery store owners considering a measure which would make see-through packaging mandatory.

As such comments became common in our daily mail in early June, we formulated a standard response for those legislators who wrote to us, based generally on our conflicts of interest policy statement.

To a casual observer of the Project, the exchange of letters and phone calls might appear unimportant. And while the tangible results of such exchanges might be hard to gauge, we believe it created one of the most constructive dialogues regarding the roles of legislators and the institutions in which they serve.

In several cases, for example, my letter in response to a comment or inquiry resulted in another letter from the legislator, for instance:

I'm glad to know more about the CCAG's citizen evaluation. It could be that were I in your position, I would approach the problem in much the same way. With more experience, I might operate differently and improve my chances of obtaining positive results. Nevertheless, a meaningful dialogue demands an exchange of views on the subject. Perhaps I can help

. . . . Whatever your motives, whomever you represent, however noble your intentions, I must (as a legislator) consider CCAG another lobby. Instead of offering free meals, you offer free headlines—good ones to the cooperative, bad ones to the uncooperative—no mention at all for those you'd rather ignore. The difference is that I *can* decline the invitation for the free meal."

Another example is the correspondence with a Representative who first wrote to us regarding financial disclosures:

Your organization is too brash and whimsical to permit me to disclose such a personal matter to you. Even if you show signs of maturity in the future, I shall not make such disclosure to you, in the absence of persuasive reasons for public benefit.

Following our response in which we asked him to produce evidence to support his subjective judgments, he wrote again:

First, I want to assure you that my remarks are not directed at any specific member of your organization. . . . Also, I firmly believe that most of your staff and your workers are serving with dedication. I am aware of the very long and hard hours with which your staff pursues the cause of public interest at low annual compensation . . . I am personally appreciative of that service. I feel also that there is much wrong with our legislative system which you will help uncover and correct and, for all these reasons, I feel that you are most deserving of our support . . . .

This Representative also explained with grace his use of "brash and whimsical" as adjectives for our group, questioned our lack of self-interest and what he termed "Marxist-sounding" statements concerning legislative salary increases:

> ... I also reject the suggestion, which I think is implicit in your statements, that perhaps those who cannot make a living privately should be encouraged to run for public office. You can be sure that I stand ready to vigorously sound the public alarm upon any further evidence that your group may have intended such Marxist meanings in your statement. . . .

I might also state that we found sympathy and encouragement for the Project among a number of legislators whose actions and remarks were wonderfully gratifying, although not quite as memorable.

At the time of our questionnaire mailing, we sought action rather than reaction from other citizen groups. We asked them if they would distribute citizen questionnaires, whether and how else they could help, and if they had any ideas to improve the ways in which we were going about the Project.

The Common Cause people hedged, hemmed and hawed, and told us they would have to consult their main office in Washington to find out if they could provide lists of people to whom we could send the questionnaires. (They had refused to help on other occasions when they could have provided lists to strengthen our Citizens' Lobby.)

After Angie Martin became almost violent with them, telling them that this was the sort of thing we groups should be working together on and that we should not have to go through such a big deal just to get information, they finally said they would probably be able to mail out some of our questionnaires. They have several thousand members in Connecticut—they took sixty questionnaires!

The best response in terms of groups was from the National Organization for Women (NOW). They were somewhat like us—less structured than some of the older and more traditional groups. Sending out the questionnaires seemed like a good idea to their leaders, and they followed through with a mailing.

Our dealings with the state office of the League of Women Voters were somewhat of a disaster all along the line. We asked first if they would distribute citizen questionnaires. No luck. Would they give us a list of local League chapters and their presidents so we could interview them concerning the responsiveness of their legislators? Again we were turned down.

"They said the League speaks with one voice," Angie told me, "even though we explained that all we wanted to know was whether or not they thought a legislator was doing a good job—aside from political considerations."

Speaking with one voice, the state League said "sorry."

Fortunately, we did make contact with several local League chapters and found enough cooperative people at this level to help us with the "service to constituents" section of the study. But once again, it was a case of a traditional organization that had evolved into a rigid structure at the top and whose primary concern seemed to be, at least to us, rules and order above all else—even above substantive accomplishments.

Certainly our experiences should not discourage others from approaching such groups (and others) in their states. Membership and leadership vary not only from area to area but from year to year. I have heard, for instance, that if we had been seeking help from the Massachusetts League of Women Voters, cooperation would have been readily available.

Digging Deep

RESEARCHING LEGISLATORS' records is usually not very exciting. Unlike other recent efforts at social change, such work has little drama. Certainly it is not like Kunen researching and writing about the "revolution" at Columbia University for *The Strawberry Statement*. Instead, our research efforts were boring beyond belief. Day after day during June, our people trudged off to the State Capitol, the State Library or the morgues of daily newspapers. The best part of the day was when those places closed!

It would be inaccurate to say that morale sank during the research period because this was where the summer workers came in—at the psychological bottom. They were welcomed to the Project with an instruction sheet on what information would be available to them as "the public." They were then assigned to a particular area such as voting records, campaign contributions or newspaper files—and pointed in the direction of the appropriate building.

After several days there were rumblings of disenchantment among these new staff members. It was not that some tasks were more boring than others—*everything* was dull.

Only the degree differed. Newspaper clippers had it just a little bit better than campaign contribution transcribers.

At first there were complaints about a lack of guidance. What they were really saying was that they could not see where the Project was going. What good would all this information do? How would it be used? Students, especially, are so accustomed to doing research that is never used for anything except an escape route to the next grade that they are wary of the whole research process.

We had told them when they arrived that the Project would produce information on legislators in time for the elections. What form it would take had not yet been determined. In fact, we ourselves were feeling our way, and the workers knew it. But we had had a sufficient glimpse of the "big picture" to insist they continue.

By mid-June, although the unhappiness and depression were still at least partly below the surface (evident more in facial expressions than in discussions of revolt), it had risen to an inner crisis which could have halted or delayed the research. There was considerable support among the summer people for holding discussions about the goals of the Project. But aside from a brief meeting, we refused to slow down. There would be no hand-holding, no dragged-out encounter sessions. It was simply a matter of getting the material together in time for interviews—in the districts and with the legislators themselves—or risking the whole Project.

Part of the problem was the expectations of the workers. Being "Nader's Raiders" for a summer had appeal, and that was responsible for our attracting some of them. But few who applied had any idea of the drudgery involved in "raiding." To many of them, it was supposed to be glamorous work that would turn the whole system on its ear. And for some reason, there were also expectations of social gatherings, beer and burger parties, and lakeside fires on lazy summer evenings. But they soon discovered that the "parties" took place at ten at night beside the office percolator during an infrequent break in key punching.

But the Nader affiliation was also one of the major reasons that the workers continued to believe in us when we said it would all be worthwhile in the end. It was Ralph's reputation of getting things done that really kept all of us going and it was unthinkable to us on the permanent staff that the Project could falter. There was too much at stake, too many commitments, too many promises to keep. We took the obstacles to our research as they came.

At first we had compiled a list of what materials were supposed to be available to the public. This was broken down for the researchers into various categories.

At the State Library:
  Floor Transcripts
  Copies of Bills
  Public Hearing Transcripts
  Voting Records
At the Capitol Committee Rooms:
  Minutes of Committee Executive Sessions
  Other Committee Records
At the Secretary of State's Office:
  Campaign Contributors
  Expenditures of Candidates
  Personal Expenses of Candidates
  List of Registered Lobbyists
From local newspapers and librarians:
  Clippings
From the Legislative Management Office:
  Travel Vouchers

We planned on researching everything available at the State Library. Especially important to us were voting records and floor transcripts. In the early stages of this portion of the Project, we also decided to log legislators' statements at public hearings and note the bills which they introduced, even though we were uncertain about the value of this material.

We found that voting records were available as expected, but these covered only roll call votes—some major bills had been passed with only voice votes and went unrecorded. But at least part of the information was there and we put our people to work compiling the available records for the past two sessions.

Including campaign contributions in each file also seemed important. This information was said to be readily available, but would have to be copied by our volunteers—for more than two hundred legislators!

This campaign spending data was accessible, but only as noted on special forms in the Secretary of State's Office. We copied a blank form, mimeographed a couple of hundred of them and our researchers filled in the information: a most dreary task taking three weeks for several workers to complete.

Newspaper articles were to be another valuable part of each legislator's "public statements" file. We planned to focus initially on the two major Hartford dailies, one of which was the largest newspaper in the state. At the same time, we began planning how to cover the other dailies and weekly papers.

When we first approached the Hartford papers, we were given specific rules regarding the use of their morgues and libraries. Few people other than reporters use these valuable sources and when they do it is generally for very short periods of time. When the newspapers realized that we wanted to look at every clipping on every legislator for the past two years, they were appropriately astonished. Our plan to copy by hand also surprised them, but xeroxing them was far too expensive a process for us.

"You'll have to tell us which clippings you'd like and we'll get them for you," was the initial response at one paper. But after two days the librarian relented and allowed our researcher access to the files. (At one paper, a worker had to sit on the floor for an entire day, copying, copying, copying ....)

For the other important dailies and weeklies we lined up volunteers in almost every community to begin the same process. A routine had finally been established and by the first week in June we felt we were under way.

Compiling some of the other material presented problems. Often what are called "public records" are not very public. In some cases there are simply no such records available, even though it is written somewhere that they exist. This was true of committee records. In planning the Project, we had decided to analyze the institution of the General Assembly as well as the records of its members. Ralph Nader had strongly suggested looking at committee performances as a way of determining how issues had been approached and handled. His Congress Project was, of course, doing this in depth.

In Connecticut the Legislative Management Office oversees legislative procedures. Its Director had been sympathetic to our work in the previous year and so we expected continued cooperation. We approached him on the committee records and were told we would be allowed access to portions of them—but the records were kept in each committee room, they were locked during "interim sessions" and this was one of those periods.

The Legislative Management Director's edict about only "portions" of the files being public both amazed and disappointed us. Although Angie Martin lodged a verbal complaint at the time, we did not challenge his decision formally. We needed his cooperation throughout the summer on other matters and there was no time to wage a "freedom of information" battle which could eventually have led to a court fight.

The rationale for denying us access to the complete files was that within them there were "personal" matters, mainly the correspondence of committee chairmen.

We finally agreed to a system whereby our researchers would contact a secretary designated by the Legislative Management Office and tell her which files we wanted to see. The secretary would then contact the committee staff member who was working during the interim session, he would notify the committee chairman, and if permission was granted, we took the necessary notes. Ah, the joys of bureaucracy!

We did find that there was greater cooperation when the same CCAG representative remained in contact with the committee secretary. It was easier for her, but it was not always possible for us.

This complicated and time-consuming procedure finally became so unbearable that near the end of the summer I wrote to the Legislative Management Director, "If these are really 'public records,' they should be readily available to the public. Neither we nor any other citizens should have to go through this weeding out process."

We probably would have pushed harder for complete access to committee records if it had appeared that they were going to be worthwhile. But we found quite early in our research that most committees simply don't keep detailed minutes. Votes were unrecorded, with rare exception, and there was no way to determine accurately who had attended the meetings. (In the public hearing transcripts, those present at the beginning of the hearing would be noted, but those who walked in later would not.)

When Ralph Nader had noted the importance of committee records, he undoubtedly had forgotten that his home-state legislature operates in a much more haphazard manner than the U.S. Congress. In June, mid-way through our research in this area, we abandoned our plans for analysis of committee performances, but our public records research continued in other fields—as did our problems with obtaining information.

At the State Library we were fortunate to have a sympathetic legislative librarian who showed us the transcripts of both public hearings and floor debates. We found them only marginally useful. It took more than three weeks for three full-time workers supplemented by volunteers to plod through the hearings on every bill and copy any significant comments which would give a good idea of how active and informed a legislator had been. If there was no mention of the legislator in the transcripts, no questions to a witness and no testimony, it indicated something. Again, this was not conclusive, especially as legislators were burdened with too many committees and could not be active on all of them. But it did furnish a guide, just as travel vouchers gave us a rough idea of the amount of time legislators spent at the Capitol.

The time invested in obtaining information from public hearing transcripts may have been better spent elsewhere, and I would advise that a general analysis of committee operations in another state be made before any specific and tedious study is undertaken.

Floor debates were something else again. These transcripts were both the most helpful to our Project and the most difficult to use. I well remember the day in early June when we learned that numerous huge volumes of verbatim transcripts for the past two years were indexed by bill number only. This made it easy to locate the volume and page, but tedious and troublesome if you wanted to gain an overall picture of the performance of a particular legislator on the House or Senate floor. An individual citizen seeking to do such analysis for one legislator's record would have to undertake a page-by-page inspection to determine if his particular legislator had spoken on a bill. In 1971 alone, the General Assembly considered more than five thousand bills!

This was one of the points during the Project when we seemed to run directly into a stone wall. Copying every significant statement made by every legislator for two sessions was out of the question. Time was running out on the first phase of the Project; we would soon have to arrange appointments for legislative interviews to take place in late July and August and, following that, most of the researchers would go into the districts to begin interviewing community leaders and constituents.

A Yale student working with us who was skilled in computer use offered to devise a system to computerize the entire record of floor debates with a printout sheet for each legislator. Thus our researchers or anyone else who wanted to look at the transcripts by legislator rather than by bill would have an annotated index. What we needed, he said, were people to key punch.

But before the go-ahead could be given, we needed copies of the transcripts to carry to the key punch machine. And at that point, the only machines to which we had access were at Yale and a couple of Hartford corporations with friendly employees. This time the Legislative Management

Office came through. They lent us their copies, the only ones in the state.

But where to find key punchers? We placed posters on bulletin boards in corporation headquarters and made Public Service Announcements on the radio. Finding such people for work on lovely summer evenings was, to say the least, not easy. Finally we threw the job to the summer staff and the few volunteers who said they were with us for the duration. For more than two weeks, sometimes far into the early morning hours, they key punched, following a detailed set of instructions labled, "How to Use Index Forms for Floor Debate in the Legislature." They read, in part:

> We would like an entry for every statement made in the Legislature except prayers, comments by the Speaker (or acting chairman) and housekeeping and procedural motions. If in doubt, err in the direction of including too much.

The rest of the two-page form contained technical instructions on how to key punch. A sympathetic computer programmer employed by a Hartford firm then had the material run through machines and the resulting printout sheets were placed in the files of the legislators.

In addition to the lawmaker's name and district, the printout contained the month and date of statement, the bill number, the subject to which he was speaking, the results of the statement (movement to adopt, to reconsider or recommit), any amendments, a summary of the statement (not to exceed 58 letters), and the page and volume of the transcript in which the statement could be found.

Looking at the printout sheets the night they were delivered, most of us had the impression for the first time in this research phase, that we had something extremely valuable. As a matter of fact, several months later when our profiles were released to the public, one of the librarians who had been friendly and helpful asked, "Why haven't we been doing that?"

The floor transcripts had been brought to life by our effort. Prior to that, their use by citizens had been limited. Reporters, legislators or legislative staff members would use them to trace a "legislative history" on a particular bill, but to approach them in search of an overall view of a legislator's performance on the floor was something new.

Toward the end of our research portion, we decided to borrow another Nader Congress Project tactic by attempting to interview legislative staff members. We wanted their impressions on the legislative process in general, but were also hoping to obtain information about the performances of individual committees and their members.

"Anybody on my staff who offers an opinion about the inner workings of the State Legislature will be fired," said one director. "I would have to let anybody go who commented on the individual committee performances," said the second.

That took care of that. In only a few instances were we able to obtain "off-the-record" comments, and chances are that if we had to do it all over again we would not go to the top first.

Near the end of June we had virtually completed all our research, and most of our initial volunteers, as well as our low-paid staff, were still with us.

I found that when I spoke to these people they seemed to remember little about that month. Most of it had been wiped out of their minds, but they all admitted that their later interaction with legislators and the final profiles could not have been possible without that dreadful homework.

Making Contact

THE DUSTY, musty record searching was over. We emerged from the libraries, newspaper morgues and an office piled with printout sheets to begin the next step of the Project—a determination of each legislator's service to constituents through interviews with community leaders, the general public and the legislators themselves.

By late June the first phone calls to legislators were about to begin with requests for interview appointments to be held in late July and early August. Everybody looked forward to this phase of the Project.

Those of us on the permanent staff who had become so accustomed to dealing with public officials did not realize what a big step it was for some of the workers. "I was so nervous when I made my first call," recalls Alexandra Woods, "that I almost forgot to ask for the interview."

Our callers were carefully instructed before making their calls to remember the following:

1. Ask if the legislator is going to run again. If not, you need not proceed, but be sure to ask if it has been made public.

We don't want to have people say they're not running and then find them on the ballot in November with no information gathered on them.

2. Ask if the legislator is willing to consent to an interview between July 25 and August 25. If yes, set the date.

   a. If the legislator says, "I need more information on the Project," refer to your outline of the Project and its goals.

   b. If the answer is, "Yes, but call me later for a specific date," explain our tight time schedule and press for a commitment.

3. If the legislator says no,

   a. Stress the importance of the interview to the overall Project.

   b. Mention that the interview provides an opportunity to elaborate on and comment on information we have collected in research. Stress that portions of the interview will be included in the published profile.

   c. State that the interview provides CCAG with suggestions on how to improve the Project.

   d. Point out that we are going to prepare a profile of the legislator anyway, so it is to his or her advantage to grant an interview.

4. If the answer is still absolutely no, obtain a reason from the legislator and take down quotes.

5. If he or she wants to do the interview sooner than July 25, point out that we would like the session to be as beneficial as possible to both us and the legislator and thus need to do adequate research first.

6. Ask the legislator if the preliminary questionnaire has been received. If it has not been returned, does he or she plan to return it? Explain that we have changed one question and are now asking for major corporate clients, not individual clients.

7. If the legislator tries to get you into a discussion of disclosure,

point out that these are the kinds of things we want to discuss in the interview. If you must, refer to our statement of policy on the matter.

8. Ask the legislator what community groups in his or her district exhibit the most interest in legislation. We want any groups, including business, PTA and the like.

9. AVOID LONG DISCUSSIONS ABOUT ANYTHING. DON'T GET INTO ARGUMENTS!

Some legislators immediately refused to grant an interview upon hearing from us. One veteran Senator said, "I took one look at that questionnaire and knew I wasn't interested in cooperating." A freshman Representative was even more blunt:

> You have no right to ask the questions that you did [on the preliminary questionnaire]. I don't want to get boxed in answering those questions. It smacks of arrogance; it's almost like a threat.

"My income is nobody's business," said another when he heard the voice of our caller. It was only after several assertions that income was only a minor part of the entire study that the legislator agreed to an interview.

We found that the semi-personal contact of a phone conversation helped reduce the hostility that had been generated by the preliminary questionnaire. Many legislators who had reacted angrily to our initial statement and questionnaire quickly granted interviews when the entire Project was explained to them over the phone. Publicity about the number of legislators who had already agreed to interviews also helped pressure some who were reluctant into setting a date. Others agreed but were clearly unhappy about it. They simply decided that it would have been worse to be labeled as refusing to talk to a citizen group. Most of those who refused completely were from "safe" districts where re-election would be no problem.

Our policy, as reflected in the instructions to our callers, was to bend over backward to convince the legislator to agree to an interview. In some cases it hurt our pride to try to calm a legislator who was screaming through the phone about how unfair and slanderous our Project had become. But we knew that the interview was going to be the most important thing. If somebody was an ogre, it would come out in the interview without our ever having to say so.

Public Servants and Private Self-Servers

ORDINARILY the average citizen does not know very much about the record of an individual legislator. Yardsticks of performance like voting records, attendance records and numbers of statements made on the chamber floor don't attract much attention. But few people forget the outcome of their own personal contact with a state Representative, his vote on a bill in which they expressed interest, phone calls returned or ignored, letters answered or forgotten, the personal promise to "look into the matter" fulfilled or broken.

Congressional representatives employ staff members as "caseworkers" to communicate full-time with constituents back home. After elections you can hear people say how surprised they are that certain Congressmen or Senators continue to survive even though they have, for instance, poor attendance records or questionable campaign contributors or anti-consumer voting records. They may even lack charisma. The answer is good casework. Even though the number of people who benefit directly from this sort of assistance is small compared to the total electorate in a district, the word seems to get around. This is one reason incumbents have such a tremendous advantage in campaigns.

If casework is important for federal legislators, it is all the more vital for state and local officials. Not only are the issues closer to citizens' lives, *they* are closer to the citizens themselves. In some places and situations the questions and complaints made to state legislators can be difficult enough to answer for the legislator with a legal or administrative background. For the bricklayer or building contractor or bartender, they often are impossible.

When people want help, they want it quickly. The need is to speak to someone who knows the scene in the State Capitol, or "downtown" in the case of a city councilman, and they prefer face-to-face or phone communication in place of a letter. This can mean virtually no privacy for the conscientious legislator. And if this type of help is unavailable, nothing else the legislator does is going to mean a thing.

Service to constituents, then, is an important performance standard when taking a hard look at a legislator's overall record. But it is also a difficult area to quantify and was the most controversial segment of our study as far as most critics were concerned.

How can such service be measured? Again relying on the Congress Project, we concentrated on two major questions: (1) How does the legislator seek to inform constituents about important issues and his views on them, and (2) How does the legislator provide opportunities for citizens to express their own opinions about those issues or others of interest to them?

The Congress Project provided a questionnaire for "community leaders" from which we drafted our own. Most of the community leader interviews were done by phone, but in some cases our researchers traveled to various towns and cities trying to determine who the community leaders were and which were most involved with state legislation.

We promised the community leaders anonymity, not only because it would make them more willing to talk, but also because disclosure of their names could mean that their effectiveness with their legislators might diminish in subsequent sessions. But later, in the profiles, we provided general descriptions such as "League of Women Voters member" or "representative of a business group" for each leader who was quoted.

Through our Citizens' Lobby we also distributed citizen questionnaires which asked people to provide information about their individual experiences with legislators. And, of course, the lobbyists themselves were valuable in furnishing information on almost every legislator in the state: they had gotten to know each other very well.

At this point we needed lists from other citizen groups to expand our coverage as far as possible, but as I mentioned earlier, they were hard to come by. For this reason, we did not have the citizen distribution we would have liked. Moreover, the people from whom we really needed to hear —those who petition or complain to their legislators—were not listed on the rolls of any organization: they are not necessarily joiners.

But we did manage to acquire enough information to make a general judgment regarding the degree of each legislator's responsiveness and this was a worthwhile segment of the Project. Our overall impression was that constituents, even community leaders, have little substantive knowledge about the records of their legislators. Contact on a specific issue, yes. But overall knowledge, no.

Informing constituents of legislative activities is indeed a necessary service, even though there is no one person calling or cajoling for a specific bill. This can be done in a number of ways—newsletters, meetings or exposure through the local press, for example. Newsletters are not as expensive as many legislators contend, yet we found attorneys making well over fifty thousand dollars per year who said there was no way they could afford a single mailing!

Ultimately the legislator must rely on the media. And there can be great differences among the media and their degree of cooperation with a legislator's effort to inform his constituents. We were warned while planning the Project that a flat judgment about the extent to which legislators sought to inform constituents must take into account the differences from paper to paper in their willingness to cooperate. For instance, a part-time aide to a progressive Representative from New Haven was concerned that we might begin comparing legislators covered by the media in entirely different ways. In a confidential memo to us he said:

Getting staff coverage from, or getting a release which meets reasonable newswriting standards, into the *Bridgeport Post*, which is a warmly generous and community-minded paper is three times as easy as breaking into the *New Haven Register*. . . there are great variations in accessibility even with the same newspapers. A city legislator generally has a tougher time breaking into print. The reason, using the *Register* as an example, is that legislative or political news from central city legislators has to go through a couple of conservative Capitol staffers who know which side 'Papa' Jackson butters their bread [Jackson owns the *Register*]—and who are working under space limitations imposed to assure that the stockholders continue to enjoy a consistent 20% plus rate of return. But, on the suburban-rural territorial pages, space allotments are much more generous, partly because these pages go into a split run only and hence the cost is less to publish. And partly also because the *Register* as well as the *Hartford Times, Courant* and other large city newspapers are promoting new circulation in the suburbs and sticks, but generally not doing so in the city.

This aide also warned in his memo that "a majority of radio newsmen really don't know what the hell they're doing most of the time." He admonished us to "keep in mind that a lot of trivia gets onto radio stations while much solider stuff never hits the air waves because of the inexperienced and poor news judgment of radio newsmen."

He may, however, have overstated the differences in exposure among legislators, although his point was well-taken. As with other criteria of performance standards, we tried not to put a disproportionate emphasis on the "service to constituents" section.

Perhaps the more important point is that most of these part-time legislators are not media magicians. Dealing with the press, writing and distributing releases, sizing up issues and planning a strategy that will include maximum press coverage is not something that comes naturally. Experience is really the best teacher. And it doesn't hurt to have some staff members who are public relations-oriented. We found that many Connecticut legislators who had not been in office long and who had no staff and little experience became bewildered, frustrated and even angry when trying to obtain media coverage of their statements. Some actually rejected the idea of seeking coverage, as if maximizing exposure were against the rules of the game. One Senator told us, "I rarely issue press releases. I don't like to manufacture news. I'm more comfortable when reporters come to me when I *make* news." This particular Senator, however, does have a weekly column in a regional "shoppers' newspaper."

A fourteen-year legislative veteran from a small factory town in eastern Connecticut said he never issued newsletters or newspaper columns, never had office hours or sponsored community forums on special issues. "I try to keep out of the press as much as possible." (He was soundly defeated in his bid for re-election, and is now very much "out of the press.")

Most legislators do not want to be out of the press, but the number of news releases they hand out and the coverage they receive vary widely from one lawmaker to the next. Those who do not hold "professional" jobs on the outside—as lawyers or businessmen—find it extremely difficult to produce releases and distribute them properly. One Representative, a thirty-nine-year-old building contractor told us his annual income was "less than ten thousand dollars per year." He does not issue a newsletter or write a column. Nor does he appear to issue many press releases. "I don't have a secretary or even a wife to do small things," he told us. He believes there should be a central office set up in each district so that legislators like himself could pool their clerical help and become more efficient without suffering financially in the process.

Columns in weekly newspapers—there are a large number of them in Connecticut—are much more common. These columns take the form of either factual accounts of legislative activity during the past week—the bills considered and their purposes—or, in some cases, more philosophical statements about the effects of the bills or the legislative process itself. In more than one instance, we reviewed legislators' columns to find they had described the bills considered during the past week without telling their constituents how they voted. The following excerpt from the weekly *Weston Forum* might be called a model; it combined the philosophical and the factual:

A state representative lives to a very great extent in a vacuum. His more fervent desire is to represent the wishes of his constituents. His handicap, however, is that he is never absolutely sure of what the majority wants. . . .In the final analysis, he must believe that he is a reasonable man and that the majority of his constituents are reasonable human beings who react to issues about the same as he does.

One woman Representative, through her column, invited her constituents to testify at public hearings at the State Capitol: "The rooms are small and uncomfortable. The wait is long. Go anyway. What you say at the Capitol can make new laws." And in another column she wrote:

One sixth grader the other day asked me, 'Is being a legislator hard work?' I've been thinking about that and why I answered 'Yes.' It is hard work because of the responsibility of being a part of the decision-making process on Capitol Hill. . . . It is hard work because of the quality of work to be done. . . . But . . . I think I'll make it.

In general, our discussions with legislators showed that only a small number actually take steps to inform their constituents about their activities, their votes, their views. Limits on time and money were frequently given as reasons for not doing so. But also mentioned by many legislators was their feeling that people really are not that interested. One Representative said he had tried newsletters and had an interesting response:

I mailed out some to my constituents but found they were unproductive and many people were most confused as to why a politician was contacting them after he was elected.

When asked how he keeps his constituents informed, another replied, "I have a big mouth."

Responding to questions on how they provide opportunities for constituents to reach them, most legislators said things like "My door is always open," "I answer all phone calls," and "They know where to find me." Office hours were something that most of them said they had tried and abandoned. "Nobody came," was the usual reply. Even people who had been conscientious in trying to keep constituents informed through news columns or newsletters said that office hours had simply not worked.

A few indicated that they regarded office hours as a bother: "I only hold public meetings when there's more than one person who cranks about something." Others expressed the view that office hours "are just a publicity gimmick."

But the few legislators who had really worked at making a success of office hours and regularly scheduled constituent meetings were anxious to talk about their worth. The most effective meetings in Connecticut are held by legislators in the Danbury area. The force behind these gatherings which are held weekly during the legislative session and monthly at other times is William Ratchford. At the time of our interview, Ratchford was Speaker of the House. With the Republican landslide in November, 1972, he was relegated to a minority leadership post.

Ratchford is known beyond Connecticut's borders as an enlightened and progressive state legislator. He has been active in national associations of state lawmakers. Along with some other Danbury area legislators, Ratchford initiated constituent meetings. When we told him of our finding that most legislators had by then dropped office hours or forums for constituents, Ratchford said:

We've found that you have to do it regularly and you have to see that it's publicized. To do it one or two times and say that it's failed? It's *going* to fail if you only do it one or two times. Secondly, we find in campaigning door-to-door, that people appreciate this who never take advantage of it.

He summarized some of the issues that had brought people to the last meeting just a few days before:

Three parents were in with children with hearing problems between the ages of three and five who have to commute to Bridgeport every day, because there is no state program nearer than that. What can we do to get the Department of Education to have a program at this end of the County? Secondly, Lake Kenosha is a neighborhood lake where we have a public bathing area. We also have a summer program for the kids who can't afford regular camps. There's been a dramatic increase in the bacteria count. What can we do to get the Department of Environmental Protection to test regularly.... We get a lot of neighborhood requests which are later translated into legislation. We had a pharmacist who said he had no means of refusing to sell hypodermic needles and syringes by the gross. There's a New York law requiring them to refuse or to require a prescription. That law was introduced in Connecticut and passed because of that.

Some legislators who do not use office hours or constituent meetings employ other means. A Representative from Hartford told us he walks through his district each Saturday, stopping to chat with people along the way. One fourteen-year veteran of the House, a stonemason, told us he prides himself on being "a working man," able to talk with people who are "not necessarily the wealthy or the poor:"

I get ridiculed because I go into the bar on Friday nights; you'd be amazed at the information you get—some people feel that's not the place where a legislator should be.

A former Assistant Majority Leader doesn't have to go to someone else's bar: he is easy to reach in his own. "For the price of a 25¢ beer, I'm here." A legislator from Colchester owns a roadside stand where, he said, people drop by to discuss legislative matters with him.

When added to the legislator's own statements about how he related to his constituents, the views of community leaders and other citizens on this point helped form an impression of the kind of job each legislator was doing in the community. Not that we found many people in each district who had knowledge of the legislator's record. But where we could meet with more than a few constituents, the cumulative information helped make generalizations.

Our own Lobby people gave the most specific examples of situations in which a legislator had either been responsive or insensitive. But most of what we learned came less from specific examples than from overall impressions.

Of the eighteen legislators who refused to cooperate in the Project, it was not surprising to find a majority had not been conscientious about serving constituents. Of a veteran of the General Assembly, the powerful co-chairman of the Banks Committee, more than one constituent complained, "I only got an answering service." He suffered a startling defeat in November.

Another sixteen-year veteran survived, however. People we spoke with in his district accused him of never returning phone calls or answering letters. "But he votes right," said one labor official.

Political philosophies appeared to make little difference in service to constituents: "conservative" members were as responsive as were the "liberals." But, in general, urban Democratic legislators from safe districts were among the least responsive to constituents.

On the other hand, one of Bridgeport's legislators could evidently not afford to ignore his district's needs: in 1970 he edged his opponent by a scant fifty votes. An anti-poverty worker told us that he was "a good local politician," and another person from the Black portion of his district said:

> Everybody seemed to think he's doing a very good job; people from all sorts of groups. He's the only white person I know that comes to meetings in this part of town. Every time there's a hot issue, he speaks up to it.

He does not issue many press releases and, even when his party was in power in Hartford, he was not in the spotlight much. He is a quiet man, but one who has apparently worked at taking care of the people in his district. He could attest to the importance of doing those little things for constituents. In November, 1972, after his profile was written and distributed, he survived the Nixon landslide and won re-election while more visible legislators had not.

One of these was a six-year veteran who represented a district which was heavily Black. She had told us about her difficulty in reaching constituents:

> My district is very unique. I couldn't go house to house, not in this neighborhood. I have no direct way of communicating with them.

We found a considerable amount of resentment against her among leaders of community groups. One of the Black community leaders told us, "She came to me once and said 'I have ten minutes. What about these housing problems.' " Up against the combination of her own record of seeming unresponsiveness and a rising Black desire for community control, she was forced to move into another district and was soundly defeated.

Likewise, there were others who survived as long as they did by compiling a good party voting record, for example, a Representative from Bridgeport with a "good vote, poor service" tab in his community. Almost all comments about his responsiveness were negative: he was one of the famous eighteen who had refused to cooperate with us. Not once in two years had he spoken on the floor of the House. But he won re-election in what is considered a relatively poor section of Bridgeport while the best comment a community leader could make about him was, "He usually shows up in time for the election."

There are legislators who serve their constituents by a steady introduction of bills relating to "hometown" issues: a request for funds to outfit the local drum and bugle corps, for example, park benches near the home for the aged, a change of traffic pattern to help downtown business. These are also special interest bills which can clog the wheels of government, but which are an easy way to re-election. The legislators who encourage such measures have a nucleus of support among the parents of the kids in the drum and bugle corps, relatives of the elderly and the local Chamber of Commerce. Whether they do nothing else for the session, they speak not a word in debate or issue a single press release, they have built-in, if not hard-earned votes.

But is this truly a service? Is it the job of the legislators to acquiesce to the desires of their constituents, or should they be voting their own consciences?

This was a question brought up during the interviews. On two issues particularly, a number of legislators said they had voted against their own consciences because of pressure from constituents—on a state income tax and enfranchisement of eighteen-year-olds.

A college professor and maverick Senator said he usually takes "a middle group position," by neither following the "Burkian concept of voting his conscience nor the poll-taking concept."

And I don't consider that a cop-out. My constituents were opposed to an income tax. But even though the message was delivered loud and clear by 800-900 pieces of mail and phone calls all through the night: "NO INCOME TAX, PERIOD!"I held out practically to the very end. I did in the end vote to repeal [the income tax], but not before I offered amendments to make the income tax more palatable to the middle class. And when I voted to repeal, I announced that it was not according to my best judgment, but that I was responding to overwhelming pressure.

A Representative from rural Litchfield also had trouble with the income tax. "I basically represent the consensus," he told our interviewer. "However, there are situations where the consensus is wrong because they don't have the information available to evaluate the situation themselves." The tax issue was just such a situation, according to his statement:

As far as I could determine in terms of sheer arithmetic and economics, approximately 72 percent of the average group that I represent would probably pay less under the graduated type of income tax than the proposed sales tax packages that were available. . . . My reaction to the poll I conducted of 10 percent of my constituents was that people do not react to something like a graduated income tax in a logical manner. They'd rather have the option of paying more under the sales tax and still have the flexibility of spending their money as they see fit. Where this is not the best thing for them in terms of dollars and cents, based on the survey, I went back and changed my vote even though I personally disagreed with that and I personally attempted to tell them.

The present House Majority Leader said he also voted against the income tax even though he personally favored it, making a distinction between issues on which a legislator can vote his conscience, "an issue that is wholly moral like abortion or capital punishment," and one like taxes where "I think the legislator is bound to follow the views of his constituents."

One Representative famous for taking polls and quoting them on the floor of the House spoke for the bill concerning a penalty for intoxicated drivers:

> I like to pass on to this body the fact that whenever possible, I feel it is my responsibility to reflect the direct opinion of my constituency; 414 voted yes and 284 voted nay in the poll, and so I vote 'Yes.'

On the no-fault insurance bill he rose once again to state: ... 552 of my constituents asked me to vote for this no-fault bill. I submit to you that this is the public speaking and I think their wishes should be considered.

He was the only Republican incumbent defeated for re-election in 1972. The public had spoken once again.

There was opposition to this point of view, however, from one who was not reluctant to assert:

I very emphatically do not subscribe to the theory that you
are to do as your constituents want you to do. If my vote is
contrary to the wishes of my constituents, they could go to
the polls in November and just vote me out. If I were to have
a referendum on every question, they don't need me—they need
a robot.

As we had assumed would be the case when planning
our Project, however, voting records were not necessarily
the most important indicator of a legislator's service to
constituents. Again and again we saw this verified by statements from both citizens and legislators as well as by ana-
lyzing those other aspects of a lawmaker's performance.

A Representative and attorney from what he calls "the
silk-stocking district of Norwalk" said that voting was not
important in most cases:

...there haven't been that many close votes...I don't think
my presence as far as voting in Hartford, except on a few
occasions, meant very much really. I think it's important to
be a state representative for the various things you can do for
people.... My main contribution is working with different
groups and giving them some relationship to the powers that
be. I spend most of my time trying to act as a representative
of people who are having trouble getting things done.

It was not uncommon in the interviews for legislators
to assert that *they* themselves were the best line of defense
against special interest lobbyists. For example, a five-term
veteran (and original carver of the Howdy Doody marion-
nette) had this to say:

I often think that the situation is that the legislator is in effect a lobbyist for the public. . . .Generally, the feeling I have is that I am the defender of the public against the lobbyists.

If legislators really are *themselves* the public at the Capitol, then what role should the average citizen play? How much citizen participation should there be? Our questions to legislators included many which touched on this subject, directly and indirectly. Among the questions concerning "service to constituents," for example, we asked each legislator: "What, if any, new channels have you established for citizen participation?" When discussing the closed-door party caucus, we asked: "Does the caucus apparatus decrease citizen participation in the decision-making process?" On secret executive committee sessions, our queries included: "Should executive session minutes and roll call vote tallies be available to the public?" And the question of financial disclosure was also one that related to citizen participation.

The question from which we received the most lengthy, frank and revealing responses was of a more general type: "Do you believe that the Legislature in general could be more open to citizen inputs or participation? In what ways?" On this question, as with many others, we attempted to obtain in addition to substantive responses a categorization of where the legislator seemed to stand on the subject. Our interviewers were instructed to label each legislator's response as one of the following:

—Definite Yes
—Passive Yes
—Possible
—No Opinion
—About enough
—Passive no
—Definite no.

God would take care of us.

It was many years later when I learned what had happened to Papa. It all stemmed from the burning of Mama's dress. After the tempestuous storm of anger had swept over the souls of Mama and Papa, there came a quiet peace to Mama. "When we obey God," Mama said, "we find a rest in our souls."

For Papa, the quiet became a deep, dark chasm of guilt — and God's apparent silence. With no one to confide in, Papa rode the country roads engulfed in the dark night of the soul. He was losing his voice and the brown taste of fear brought the blackness of despair.

He had two young children to feed — Margaret (me) and Bernice — but he couldn't preach. With his voice gone, he had to leave the pulpit. He had failed!

Practical Bestemör Bertilda, who had ridden through the storms in her own life, offered the obvious solution — come home to Brooklyn.

So it came to pass that we arrived in Brooklyn. Again there was the stoic, practical advice from Bestemör, "If you can't preach, Elius Tweten, then do what you can do." That's why Papa took the job as a watchman, the guardian of a building during the long shadows of the night.

His books were set aside. His dreams were gone. Despair replaced hope. In God's apparent silence, Papa lost not only hope, but also his faith in God. Everything he had preached seemed meaningless. Each night became just one step after the other — without purpose, without meaning. Papa's Bible lay untouched on the desk.

The battle to believe was lost.

One night Mama turned the pages of her worn Bible and stopped at Job. "Lift up thy face unto God . . . make thy prayer unto Him and He shall hear thee" (Job 22:26,27), she read. "He knoweth the way that I take: when He hath tried me, I shall come forth as gold" (Job 23:10).

Turning familiar pages again she read in the Psalms:

"My soul, wait thou only upon God; for my expectation is from Him — my rock . . . my salvation . . . my strength . . . my refuge — is all in God" (Psalm 62:5-7).

The house was still. Bestemör and the children were asleep. Papa was at work. Wrapping a robe around her, Mama fell to her knees. "Lord Jesus, You said, 'If ye abide in Me, and My words abide in you, ye shall ask what ye will, and it shall be done unto you' " (John 15:7).

While the world was wrapped in darkness, Mama stayed on her knees until the beams of the morning sun dispelled the darkness and the light of God's promise broke through her despair.

She had battled against an unseen enemy who was waging a war to destroy God's servant. But Mama had a covenant with God — a covenant to walk in obedience — and God's covenant with Mama was that her household would be taught of the Lord.

She knelt beside the bed and would not give up until she heard God speak to her through His Word. "If you can believe, you'll see the glory of the Lord!" (See John 11:40.) "The LORD your God which goeth before you, He shall fight for you" (Deuteronomy 1:40).

The Word of God was welling up within her soul. She had meditated on the Word night and day, and now the Word was returning to renew her faith. "When the enemy shall come in like a flood, the spirit of the LORD shall lift up a standard against him" (Isaiah 59:19).

"As for Me, this is my covenant with them, saith the LORD; My spirit that is upon thee, and My words which I have put in thy mouth, shall not depart out of thy mouth, nor out of the mouth of thy seed, nor out of the mouth of thy seed's seed, saith the LORD . . . forever!" (Isaiah 59:21)

Deep within her, Mama heard the words of Jesus when He stilled the storm on Galilee: "Peace be still!"

Man lies before the Lord
Like the sea beneath the wind.
Faith hears the approaching
Footsteps of God's salvation.

Mama arose from her knees, dressed quickly and put on the coffee pot. The battle to believe had been fought and won!

When she turned around at the sound of footsteps she saw Papa. His face was glowing! For the first time in weeks, he stood tall and erect, head held high.

He spoke in a clear voice, "Mama, I believe God! 'Though He slay me, yet will I trust Him' [Job 13:15]. In the night God spoke to me: 'Fear thou not; for I am with thee' [Isaiah 41:10]. Mama, all the words I have given to others came flooding back to me. I know God will guide us, and I will proclaim God's Word as long as I live! My books! I must get back to my books — and my Bible, the Book of Books!" He was smiling when he added, " 'Forever, O LORD, Thy Word is settled in heaven' " [Psalm 119:29].

Papa's faith — and Papa's voice — had returned!

So that, as it was told those many years later, was why we had gone from Woodville, Wisconsin, to Bestemör's flat in Brooklyn.

Now I was remembering again those long-ago days when I came home from the contagious ward in the hospital. I was three and a half years old. My head hurt and the pain in my ears increased. Bestemör rocked me when she could, but there was the new baby, Grace.

One afternoon after coffee, Bernice crawled up into Papa's lap. She dipped her sugar lump in Papa's coffee and slowly munched on a piece of Jule kakke. "Göt, göt (good, good)" she murmured, as she laid her head against Papa's shoulder.

Terror gripped him when he felt her hot cheeks against his face. Shortly he was on his way to the contagious hospital with two-year-old Bernice wrapped in a blanket.

As they left, Mama clutched baby Grace in her arms. Bestemör moved quietly about and put on the coffee pot. She, too, was feeling the fever and the choking pain in her throat, but with a fierce determination, she doctored her throat with Lysol and peroxide and willed herself to live.

This was no time to die, not now. She had left her own young children in Norway many years ago when Joe was five and Elvina four. Now she had them near her. Elvina needed her. This time she would not fail. She would live! No one would know, until years later, of her battle with the dread disease. She moved through those grim days weak, sick, but with a passion to survive.

Day after day, Papa went to see Bernice behind the glass cubicle just as he had visited me. Then the day came when Papa came home from the hospital the last time — alone. Two-year-old Bernice was dead.

It was January, 1920 — a cold, bitter day — when they buried my sister. Uncle Joe and Pastor Hansen went with Papa — three lonely men following a tiny casket. They walked in silence, bracing themselves against the January winds, their boots crunching across the frozen ground. One man stood on each side of Papa as the cold winds blew snow over Bernice's freshly dug grave.

The kitchen was warm when Papa came home. Bestemör had the coffee pot on and Papa's sugar lumps ready. He didn't seem to notice. His eyes went to Mama rocking quietly in the corner. Mama looked up questioningly at Papa, but her words didn't come.

"Ja, Mama," he said softly. "I put the woolen socks on Bernice — and the blanket."

She nodded, overcome, then turned to nurse baby Grace.

I sat by the window, my face pressed against the window pane — staring up into the evening sky, yearning for my sister. At last I knew that God had just made an exchange. He took Bernice but gave us Grace.

Grief-stricken, Papa immersed himself in his books.

Deep within he never really forgave himself for his uncontrolled anger that might have reached Bernice, the unborn child in Mama. The golden-haired Bernice would be a constant reminder of Heaven — and man's frailty, as dust, on this earth.

Mama, too, grieved alone with her face turned to the wall. Slowly, through prayer, she climbed the mountain of faith and knelt at the cross crying out, "My help comes from the Lord."

Bestemör, Mama's mother, was acquainted with a lonely, hidden sorrow of her own that was shared with no one. Always before, she had willed strength within herself to fight life's battles alone. She did so once again.

All these things I understood much later, but, I, too, grieved alone. My sister, my best friend, was gone. As I sobbed in my pillow, the pain in my head increased.

Finally, a quiet peace fell over the household, the kind of peace only God can give.

Yet the pain in my ears continued, until I was once again wrapped in a blanket and on my way to the hospital. My severe ear infection resulted in a mastoid operation and many painful visits to the doctor's office.

I remember the cold rubber apron on the doctor's lap when he irrigated my infected ear with a solution.

Night after night Papa walked the floor with me, preaching and singing, until I fell asleep, until I was finally well.

It was more than a year after Bernice's death when we waved good-bye to Bestemör. We were leaving New York City and catching a train to Winnipeg, Manitoba, Canada, where Papa would preach again.

10

Minnesota, 1985

DURING A RADIO INTERVIEW at Northwestern College in Minnesota, I shared stories from my first book, *First We Have Coffee*. Later, phone calls came from people who remembered Mama and Papa from the Winnipeg years. Our dear friends Bill and Wilma Swanson brought us all together around a beautifully set table for "coffee."

Again our grandson Shawn heard the stories from the past. He was especially intrigued about the story of Johnny Johnson and Bjarne Hoiland when they walked eighty miles in a sixty-below-zero Canadian winter to get to the Tweten parsonage for Christmas Eve.

Tonight Johnny's lovely daughter told about her parents and their devotion to God and family. Pastor Hansen's daughter, Esther, was also remembering with us, and shared the last years and homegoing of our old friend,

Pastor Otto Hansen. Later we visited Ruth Hansen in a retirement home and shared the tears and laughter of another day. She was still as beautiful as we remembered her. Mama used to say, "Ruth Hansen is a real lady!"

Mrs. Linderholm from Winnipeg was visiting her daughter, Sylvia, and just happened to hear the radio interview. This beautiful eighty-seven-year-old lady remembered long-ago times. Ellen Locken, as a young missionary, had been in our home and in Papa's church. Tonight she sat with her handsome husband recalling many, many years in Africa.

As the stories flowed back and forth, I heard about Papa's unfailing kindness to people in need, how he was admired for his dignity in the pulpit and how he was loved for preaching the Word of God. He was respected for his total integrity.

I kept hearing words like, "Ja, your Papa was not easy to live with, stubborn and difficult; but your Mama always kept a happy household." Or, "We had a good time in your home. Stubborn, he was — but also stubborn for good."

"I remember when my husband was in the big woods, and I was expecting a baby," Mrs. Linderholm told me. "The walk to church was long and I dreaded the long walk home after church." Her eyes sparkled as she said, "Margaret, your Mama just said, 'Come, Mrs. Linderholm, have some good soup and bread with us and then we'll take a nap. The walk home won't seem so long.' "

I felt proud of my parents as Mrs. Linderholm continued, "So on Sundays I went to your parents' home and had Sunday dinner; then we took a nap. You and Grace cuddled up to me and baby Gordon slept in your mother's arm. We all took a nap together. Before I returned home we had a cup of coffee. The walk was easy then. Later, when my baby was born, I was too sick to eat but your Mama made custard and fed me until my strength returned."

She squeezed my hand. "During those hard days we

had little money and food was scarce. Someone offered a crate of free eggs for me to sell but I had no way to get the eggs. Your Papa heard about it and rode his bicycle to get the eggs. Then he balanced the crate of eggs on the bicycle and walked another five miles to bring the eggs to me. Ja, he was stubborn!"

We laughed together and recalled how my young friend, Evelyn, called me the "wild one," when we played house and made believe as only six-year-old girls can do. Our playhouse was an old shed where I managed to organize a drama department with plenty of parts and action for everyone.

One thread ran through our memories of Papa — the cord of love and God's faithfulness. Somehow we understood the frailties of the man — the angry, stubborn man — yet we saw the goodness of God in his life as well as God's care for the Twetens in those growing-up years.

As I travel around the country, I come into contact with people who have been blessed through my parents' hospitality. The most common expression seems to be, "Your father invited us home to Mama for coffee, where we laughed at his stories and felt a warm welcome."

As I share my experiences, I urge my listeners to do what Mama and Papa did — open their homes to strangers. I tell them, "The gift of hospitality is a gift from the heart. Offer that gift to God."

After Winnipeg, there was Papa's missionary work in Saskatchewan (where I helped Papa pitch the tent), then his ten years in Chicago, on to his pastorate in Brooklyn, New York, and finally, at the age of eighty-three, his retirement in Florida.

The years roll into one when remembering, but during those years Mama and Papa's children were fighting their own battles to believe. Respect for Papa, the servant of God, and the office of his ministry was instilled into us at an early age. "Touch not the Lord's anointed," Mama would say. "Guard your lips when daring to criticize a

Christian leader."

The Tweten children dared not disgrace the ministry, not as a matter of personal pride, but in order to avoid bringing dishonor to God. Discipline for us was a way of life.

When Papa was in his place behind the pulpit, Mama and her children sat with reverent awe. Papa was entrusted to bring forth God's Word to his people. Mama's children would show respect for the high calling in Christ Jesus. But the "humanity" of God's servant became the challenge for Mama's children.

After I spoke at a Christian college one day, a professor came to me with this statement, "The chapter 'Voted Out,' in *First We Have Coffee,* has meant a great deal to our students. Sometimes we have a tendency to glorify the ministry and fail to teach future leaders that being rejected can come in many forms. Even a godly man can be destroyed and not only the minister, but also the rest of the family."

I thanked the professor for his insight, and for his encouragement to me to recall even painful events to the glory of God. Even in these, we are all kept by the power of God.

Looking back over the years, the "disgraceful" event of being "Voted Out" was in retrospect a result of changing social times. The Norwegian services were voted out as the people demanded an "all American" church. Some of the elderly desired the Norwegian but the majority felt that changes were necessary. It was not the "disgrace to the ministry" that Mama's children dreaded.

Disgrace comes when leaders turn away from the truth of God's Word and preach another gospel, or become victims of the passions of immorality, or succumb to financial indiscretion. However, even in these tragic situations we desperately need men of wisdom and compassion to deal with the fallen leaders and their families — especially the children. In these tragedies, Papa believed that

God's love reached into the depths as well as the heights — that we all begin again. To Papa that was what the gospel was all about!

I had learned from Papa and Mama that the letter of the law, without the spirit of love, could destroy the faith of many people. They taught me that love without truth is not enough, but truth without love can be destructive. They wanted the church, the body of believers, to view one another as part of the family who needed each other. Mama and Papa knew that truth with love could bring the healing restoration. Papa had read more than once that Samuel told Saul to "stand still that I might show thee the Word of God."

When Papa was voted out, he retreated quietly from the "seeming rejection," but he did not lose his faith! He lived in the Word of God, but he couldn't cope realistically. He was numb!

Mama, with quiet strength, went to work as a maid. Each of the Tweten children contributed small earnings. Through it all, we learned the source of our strength — God. God didn't fail yesterday and we knew He wouldn't fail us today.

The weeks passed like the days and hours do — just one step after the other. Then the day came when the Tweten family moved to Brooklyn, New York. Papa would preach again. I remained in Chicago working as a nurse.

Bestemör Bertilda was overjoyed. After all these years, her children — Uncle Joe and Mama — were both close to her, and she could watch the rest of the grandchildren grow.

Once more Papa was in his place behind the pulpit — this time, the pulpit of The First Norwegian Baptist Church of Brooklyn, New York.

11

I'm Crying, Lord

1986!

THE GLOW OF SUNSET *casts a blend of shadows and golden light across the beautiful Lake Barkley, nestled in the hills of Kentucky. From my lodge window I look longingly at the rocky island in the center of the lake. In my mind I see a "safe place." I have just closed Gordon MacDonald's book,* Restoring Your Spiritual Passion. *How easy it would be to sing "Holy, Holy, Holy, Lord God Almighty!" on that "safe" island.*

If I could row a boat to the island, then I could find that "still" place. MacDonald had said, "By laying an adequate roadbed in the inner spirit, we can prevent the hostile elements that cause fatigue."

I am fatigued.

Too soon the shadows creep over the golden shafts

*of light and my island is shrouded in a blanket of night.
The world around me sleeps.*

Finally, I fell asleep hearing 350 women singing the
Women's Retreat song — "Holy, this place is holy. Come
now and feast on His Word." It had been a beautiful time
of sharing with God's precious people. Now it was time
for a "safe" place.

David the psalmist said he didn't understand the evil
around him until he went into the sanctuary, then he saw
from God's perspective, in the light of eternity. I was to
walk by faith, in the light of His Word.

After a night of rest I awakened to a new day and
pulled back the drapes. A thick wall of morning mist
covered the outside world. "But, Lord, I know the lake
is there," I said. "I know the hills are there — and my
island."

I sat by the window and wrote words, but my mind,
kept reaching for the hidden island. I wrote: *I know it is
there. I saw it yesterday!* In my heart, I was saying,
"Great is Thy faithfulness today, Oh God — because I
knew it yesterday."

Now I found myself thinking of another yesterday,
when I spoke at a retreat in Palm Springs, California.

As I faced eleven hundred black women, my white
hair stood out in sharp contrast to the beautiful color
around me. Their songs of praise filled the ballroom of
the luxury hotel and "Amazing Grace" took on new meaning.

Out of my heart I told about Lena, my lovely black
friend, who had said, "Unclog the channel, Margaret! You
can't see God for all the long hair and bare feet clogged
up in the channel."

Back then my channel was clogged with unanswered
questions: "Why is our son a prodigal? What did we do
wrong?" The cares of this world — with long hair and
bare feet — kept my channel clogged. I wanted "out of

the storm" — I wanted to go home.

Eleven hundred women listened intently as I told them about Lena and our son.

"If God had wanted you to die for that child, He would have asked you." Lena had scolded, "Who you be to tell God Almighty He didn't do enough when He sent Jesus to die for that child? Jesus came to give life — and that your joy be full. Now I asks you, Margaret, where is your joy? Your joy is Jesus. Your peace is Jesus. Your life is Jesus — and it does not depend on answered prayer or your family being right. *You* must get the joy of the Lord in *your* soul, Margaret. Leave the rest to God."

I looked over that sea of shiny black faces. "Lena was right, you know. She made me realize how praise unclogs the channel and, like a detergent, cleanses the cobwebs of the mind. With the channel clear I saw a sovereign God at work, bringing the 'all things together for good'! Praise was the believing before the seeing. God promised 'If you can believe, you'll see the glory of the Lord.' "

I continued, "Our children — yours and mine — are held hostage by the enemy. We as God's children, the church, must put on the armor of God and stand in the gap to intercede for these imprisoned children of ours. They are held hostage by America's permissive society that deifies man rather than God, and that has given the enemy free reign through drugs, alcohol and unbridled promiscuity. God's laws have been broken and 'the wages of sin is death, but the gift of God is eternal life' " (Romans 6:23).

Now and then a dark head bobbed with understanding. Momentarily my eyes locked with the deep, dark eyes of one lone woman. *Did she have her own prodigal?* I wondered. "We don't wrestle against a drug pusher, but we wrestle against the powers of darkness." My voice was firm. "A real Satan seeks to steal, destroy and to kill — and comes 'as a roaring lion seeking to devour'

our children."

Out of my heart I told the story of our prodigal son who came back to his heavenly Father's house. The battle to believe had been fought — and won! Eleven hundred women stood to their feet to rejoice over one sheep who had returned to the fold.

It was a high moment of faith.

The following day a message was given by another woman, a tall, dignified black woman who was known as one who interceded before the throne for the broken, wounded ones.

This woman of prayer faced the crowd with words, "When you pray, forgive." It was Lena's same theme of unclogging the channel.

With tears, the woman spoke of broken hearts and lost dreams and cried out to the sea of faces before her, "Many of you have known rejection, abuse, molestation, beatings and rape. You have lived with guilt and deep bitterness because life was unfair."

She held us spellbound. "Many lost our innocence as very young children and saw too much sin for our young years. Many went from house to house and never knew a home. It's time to cry! Cry to the Lord! Pour it all out! Be healed by your tears and cleansed by the precious blood of Jesus."

There was a rhythmic beat to her voice. "Jesus came to set us all free — cleansed, forgiven, healed and free. We begin again for in Christ all things become new. Cry unto the Lord! He hears the cry of the humble in heart."

Then I heard a sound I had never heard before — the sound of crying unto the Lord. "Tell it to Jesus," she continued. "Cry it out to the Lord. Forgive everyone who harmed you. Don't hold the hate — cry it out. Everyone has something to cry about. God hears your cries."

The sobs filled the ballroom of the luxurious hotel. Outside, the palms waved in the California sun while the birds sang. Inside, it was like the sound of the mourning of the ocean rolling on the beach. Wave after wave washed on the shore of memory. Above the sobbing came a lonely cry, like the cry of a wounded animal. "Cry, my sister. God is listening. Forgiveness is the only way — love and forgive."

I felt my own tears washing my cheeks. "Oh Lord, I'm crying, too. I'm crying with my sisters and I'm crying to You. I'm crying because I don't want to go back to the past. I only want to walk with You into the future, secure in Your love."

I, too, was remembering and weeping for the fallen leaders, oaks that crashed in the forest. Satan shouted, "Timber!" — and they fell. Dry rot was hidden in the heart of the oaks. Truth, not acted upon, had become dry rot.

I cried as I remembered angry Peter cutting off a man's ear in the garden. "The man refused to hear what You were saying, Jesus. But then Peter didn't hear either, that is, until the rooster crowed. Then he wept."

How many of us really hear You, Lord, I wondered, *or do we cut off the ears of those who don't listen to us?*

I was crying for leaders who, like Judas, turned away from walking with the Light of the world, only to go out into a night of darkness. How could love of money be so overpowering? And my tears were for their children who stumbled in the shadows.

I heard the speaker say, "Cry to the Lord." *And I cry, Lord, to You for the great men who sold their souls to their Bathshebas and turned to passion, forgetting the wives of their youth. Their children cry in the night.*

How are the mighty fallen so deep! I weep for those who once held high the Word of God, who walked with true wisdom, then turned aside to walk with vanity of pride in man's knowledge. Their children wander, without a sure compass for life's journey.

Oh, Lord, I don't want to remember the past because

I know You have forgiven and forgotten. But I must go back and perhaps help some who can't forget. Only when I walk into the past with forgiveness can I walk into the future with understanding love.

I can hear Lena singing: "So many falling by the wayside; please help me to stand."

Tears stain this page, Lord, so take my hand and let us remember together — with love.

Out of the past I allowed myself to see my brother Gordon coming home — a twelve-year-old boy, hair disheveled, coat buttoned wrong, holding out fifty cents in his grubby hand. His eyes were shining with pride, head held high. The money represented his worth for that moment, his offering of love from the sale of newspapers. His sisters crowded around him proudly. This was Gordon's moment in the sun. Not only was he on the honor roll as a student, but he also paid for his violin lessons by cleaning the basement for his music teacher. At 4 A.M. he was up and out on the Chicago streets to sell newspapers.

Now he stood facing Papa with his fifty cents gleaming in his newspaper-stained hands. Without warning, the storm broke! Papa saw only the grubby hands and disheveled appearance. Papa didn't see the worth of his son. He couldn't tolerate the lack of neatness. Papa could not risk Gordon's appearance disgracing the ministry. With uncontrolled rage, Papa's hand came down and Gordon's fifty cents flew across the room.

Then the silence!

Bruised in spirit, soul and body, our brother Gordon retreated to the only corner he knew — a cot in the dining room, with a brown box that held his earthly treasures.

The sisters clung fearfully to one another, silently screaming, "I hate you, Papa!" It was the inaudible scream of the wounded.

Papa whirled and retreated to his study. Lost in his books, his storm passed with the night.

But the storm still raged for Gordon. Beaten, bruised,

but not broken, Gordon arose the next morning to the sound of horses' hoofs and the rattle of the milk wagon. Quietly he went out into the semi-darkness to deliver his newspapers. Bitterness crept into his soul.

Sunday morning came and Papa was in his place, faithfully preaching the truth of a Heavenly Father's love. Mama's children sat in a row — but they couldn't hear Papa's words.

Back in the ballroom in Palm Springs, the focus on Gordon blurred. *Oh, Lord, I'm crying out to You again but not just for Gordon. I weep for all the leaders' broken wives and children who have been beaten with slashing words as cruel as rods. There are tears also for the leaders, those who have toppled in the forest because of slashing wounds from family or associates.*

Words have the power of life or death. Words can make men soar to heights, or can cause them to stumble, wounded, by the wayside. So many of Your children, Lord, wait for the oil and time to heal the hurting places.

I had experienced so much of the oil and wine of healing for my own hurts. Perhaps it had been easier for me, the oldest Tweten, because I became a committed Christian at six — not perfect, but committed. As I grew older, I stood up to Papa's anger, gutsy and confident — but all the while loving him. I could forgive Papa's anger because I had learned at Mama's knee to keep short accounts with God.

The lovely black leader was closing the Palm Springs meeting in prayer. With my eyes shut, I thought, *I should cry for You, too, Lord. You were counting on Your servants — weren't You?*

Tonight I pray for the children who lost their faith along the road. Tonight I thank You for helping Mama's children to go back — and now we can bring the healing we received to others. We love you, Lord.

Thank You for listening. You understand. You were beaten, too. With words and with rods.

12

I'm Singing, Lord

THE MIST LIFTS SLOWLY over Lake Barkley, bringing to my island visibility in the morning sun.

In my mind I row out to the rocky island to a make-believe hide-away. It is in the still place where I see from eternity's point of view. It is in the still place where I can hear, then my heart can sing, the "song of the soul set free."

Because I sing from a heart of joy, I can return again and again to another time with deep thanksgiving in my heart. I'm going back, Lord. Clinging to Your hand, I'm going back.

It was a lovely summer afternoon in 1946. I had taken our young children Jan and Dan for a walk in the park. Upon returning, I spotted a strangely familiar figure that came right out of my childhood, sitting on the porch. With a cry of joy, I recognized my old friend. "Uncle Barney," I called. Barney was a big, balding man — still a handsome romantic with bright brown eyes. In our carefully guarded Tweten home, Uncle Barney was our touch with "the world out there." Often he would wear a hat slouched to one side like a gangster and flash us an impish, wicked grin as he spun his yarns and sang his songs in his rich tenor voice.

Within moments we were all laughing and talking together. Jan and Dan were on his knee and he was singing, "I'm coming back to you, my hullabaloo." Uncle Barney and I laughed at the memory of Mama kneading her bread faster and faster as the songs became "too vorldly."

When Mama's glasses fell down on her nose, Barney knew it was time to softly croon a Norwegian song. The tempo of kneading slowed down as the Norwegian song blended with Mama's memories of her oceanside home at Lista, Norway.

Jan and Dan clamored for more songs, just as Mama's children used to do. Uncle Barney sang, "Just Molly and me, and baby makes three; We're happy in our blue heaven."

While I prepared supper, Uncle Barney spun his make-believe stories and the children begged for more. Harold returned from the church office and we sat around the table, once again sharing the memories of another day. Long after Jan and Dan were asleep, we still recalled that other day.

"Your father was a great man, Maggie." Uncle Barney told me. "Few understood him. Perhaps I loved your Papa the most because he had the capacity to forgive the most."

A lonely sadness seemed to linger in our old friend and the lyrics from an old familiar song . . . "Someone slipped and fell. Was that someone you?" . . . seemed to haunt me. Uncle Barney leaned forward. "My life was a total disaster when I came to your home in Canada.

Margaret, it was your father who prayed for me and I surrendered my life to Jesus Christ. Your home became my home. I loved you Tweten children more than anything in this world."

"I know," I answered, "and at one time or another we all wanted to run away with you, especially when Papa's temper exploded." I paused. "Doris was always ready to run away."

Barney was pensive. "Perhaps I knew him better than anyone, yet there was a part of your father he never shared with anyone. He spoke very little about his childhood and always kept the deep things of his heart hidden."

"Did that explain his temper?" I asked.

"Temper?" he mused. "Maggie, I've been a wild one in my day, and I know the world, the flesh and the devil. But I must say that I never knew a man so untouched by the evil in the world. Your father was a pure man — a godly man, and a man of great compassion."

I nodded. I knew Papa was a godly man. *But why that temper?* I wondered again.

"Your Papa never condoned sin, but he never condemned the sinner. I know, I know — you could never understand his uncontrolled temper. Neither could I." Uncle Barney looked away for a moment. "When I tried to talk to him, he changed the subject, or suddenly had to go someplace. He was a restless man, Maggie. I could never understand why. He had a wonderful wife — an angel — and you children were good, obedient and studious. None of you caused grief in the family. Oh, you were all very independent and probably could have gone in many directions. Now, I don't understand much, but perhaps the fear of your father kept everyone in line until you were old enough to be wise and choose God for yourselves.

"Then again, your love for your mother kept you all close. Few families are as closely knit together as the Tweten bunch." Uncle Barney smiled at Harold and me. "You can see I loved him. Your Papa saved my life, you know."

Harold and I waited quietly for Barney to go on.

"Every one of us fights a lonely battle — some a power battle or an emotional battle like your father did, and then some of us mortals have the conflict with a beautiful Delilah. We all have our Bathshebas, one way or another. I thought I was strong, but I, too, came to the place of such guilt that I couldn't face living another day. Your father understood me."

Uncle Barney looked directly at me. "That night on the Brooklyn bridge, the blackness of despair all around me, I knew I couldn't live with my agony of soul. It was then that your father came and put his arm around me and said, 'Come, Barney, let's go home for a cup of coffee.'

"We walked off the bridge together. There was no condemnation from your Papa, only love and a new beginning." Uncle Barney wiped his eyes. "You see, I loved him. He saved my life. That is the part of him you must hold to."

I never saw Uncle Barney again. He and his wife Mildred continued to minister with their special love until Barney died years later in a tragic fire.

But he helped me to remember to "hold to the good," and to leave the mystery of life's battles and question marks in God's hands.

Again as I look longingly across Lake Barkley to my rock- enclosed island, the sun rises over the hills in triumph over the darkness. Just so, each one of Mama's children came through their own darkness to rejoice in that song of the soul set free.

When I was a young child, Mama would sit beside my bed and ask, "Margaret, is there anything you need to ask forgiveness for?"

Then we would pray together over the little sins that so "easily beset us." I learned early to keep those short accounts with God. I also learned, very early, to forgive — especially to forgive Papa in regard to the rag doll. Mama taught me a bedrock foundational truth that I have since learned to understand in even greater measure.

I recall one event when Papa's unreasonable anger was vented toward me. I was a high school student and the anger rolled up into a flame within me. For a moment, I had only one desire — to lash back in fury at Papa.

But when I saw the tears running down his cheeks, the fury in me left. Slowly, I put my arms around him and said, "Papa, I love you."

But the ability to forgive had begun long before that. As a six-year-old child I walked the aisle in the Winnipeg auditorium to stand before Dr. R. A. Torrey. "I want to give my heart to Jesus," I told him.

The reality of God's love for me never has left me!

From Oswald Chambers I read: "In external history the cross is an infinitesimal thing; from the Bible's point of view it is of more importance than all the empires of the world. We have to concentrate on the great point of spiritual energy — the cross — to keep in contact with the center where all the power lies, and the energy will be let loose."

One by one, Mama's children came to the cross where the redemptive love of God through Jesus Christ became a reality. There were still unsolved mysteries, but the one thing we understood was that each one comes to the cross alone to make a personal decision to accept God's "so great salvation" — regardless of the messenger. God's plan is perfect. Somehow it comes through, even through imperfect messengers.

Each one of the Tweten children had to face the truth of God's Word and make a personal decision. At six I believed that God so loved Margaret that He gave His only begotten Son, that if Margaret believed in Him, Margaret would not perish, but Margaret would have eternal life.

Belief came to each one — for God so loved Grace, God so loved Gordon, God so loved Doris, God so loved Joyce, and God so loved Jeanelle.

That is just the beginning for all of us. After that we build ourselves up in the most holy faith. Then the battle begins!

One by one, we come to understand what Paul prayed for in Ephesians 1:17-19: "That the God of our Lord Jesus Christ, the Father of glory, may give unto you the spirit of wisdom and revelation in the knowledge of Him — [to know] the hope of His calling . . . riches of . . . His inheritance . . . exceeding greatness of His power . . ."

Into each of Mama's children came a hunger and thirst for knowing God.

St. Augustine, after his conversion, saw that the Scriptures were not words to be interpreted; they were words that interpreted their reader: "There can be no holiness apart from the work of the Holy Spirit — in quickening us by grace to Christ, and in sanctifying us — for it is grace that causes us to even want to be holy."

One day we met a man who became a spiritual father to us — a gentle, white-haired man whose face shone because he walked with God. Mr. James Mason! Mr. Mason was a tall, kindly man with clear blue eyes and the wisdom of an ancient patriarch.

He wept with those who wept, he sat with those who couldn't walk, he walked with the weak. He taught us all that the power of the Holy Spirit was the redemptive work of God being manifested in the market place. He quoted Scriptures freely, saying, "When you stand praying, forgive."

"Keep yourselves, little children," he said over and over again. "Abide in me. Let the Word of God dwell in you richly with all wisdom and spiritual understanding." And always he would remind us, "We are in a battle, not against personalities, but against spiritual darkness and a real enemy who seeks only to destroy God's people."

Because Mama's children searched the Scriptures, they desired only to walk in obedience to God.

Grace, always composed and efficient, came through her battle with darkness into the glorious light of a soul set free. Because of her struggle, she reaches out to others to show them a better way.

Gordon grew in knowledge and the wisdom of this world — a scholar in Greek and Hebrew, successful in business, but with a cool cynicism and aloofness from Papa. Gordon's heart was still numb with hurt from his childhood. He was young when he met Christ — but he came home from the military service with spiritual indifference. When God worked a miracle in our own prodigal's life, Gordon was deeply influenced.

Then the mystery of the grace of God, the work of the Holy Spirit, exploded into reality in Gordon's life. Love and forgiveness wept its way across the years to the heart of Papa when Gordon said, "I forgive you and I love you." That love poured out into every area of Gordon's life and reached out to bless his sisters.

A reunion with Gordon and his wife Alice became a praise gathering. In my mind I can still hear him singing:

"The spirit of the Lord
Is now upon me
To open prison doors
And set the captive free,
To open blinded eyes
And cause the blind to see.
The spirit of the Lord
Is now on me."

Our theme song became, "Oh come let us adore Him!"

Gordon sang the song of the soul set free!

Doris, with her spirit of determination, went off to Wheaton College with one hundred dollars in her purse.

"I need work *now,* or I won't eat!" she declared.

So she cleaned the homes of the faculty.

"I need a winter coat *now,*" she declared.

Doris found fifty dollars in her mailbox for the material, and while others made pajamas, Doris's Home Ecomomics teacher helped her sew a winter coat.

Doris marched to her own music of dedicated determination.

Then came the day when she sang a new song — the song of the soul set free — free to love and forgive and reach out with compassion. "I can do all things through Christ" is now her theme.

Joyce Solveig, the insecure, frightened one, was sensitive to the storms around her but secure in Mama's lap. Finally, she turned to her own refuge in the time of storm — the Word of God. "Fear thou not, for I am with thee" (Isaiah 41:10).

Today her song is "Through it all, Through it all, I've learned to trust in Jesus . . ." Now she sings the song of the soul set free.

Jeanelle, the youngest, was the one closest to Papa's heart. She was the child he held on his shoulder through her nights of illness.

When the rest of us left home, Jeanelle stayed close to Mama's heart in a covenant with God. Together Mama and Jeanelle believed God for miracles. Jeanelle held Papa's hand with quiet understanding but grieved over what he could have been. Through shadows and valleys, Papa's youngest has learned a deep walk with God, and she, too, sings the song of the soul set free.

Each one of us has come through dangers, toils, snares and tears. But we all arrived safely through God's matchless amazing grace. North, South, East and West you can hear us singing our song — the song of the soul set free. Hallelujah — hallelujah! The song of the soul set free.

13

The Cedar Chest, 1986

AT 6 A.M. WE WERE AT the Wilmington Airport again. This time I was heading for the snow-covered plains of Minnesota. My husband Harold checked the bags and waved good-bye as I boarded the jet. Harold would turn homeward to the typewriter and tablefull of manuscript pages. I could visualize him praying for the gift of interpretation when he viewed my hasty scrawl.

Mama had always said, "Ja, ja, you do what you have to do." For me, that was writing on yellow pads in the airports, on planes or at a kitchen table at 4 A.M.! Even now, a yellow pad rested on my lap as I leaned back against the cushioned seat. But I didn't write. My thoughts danced and sparkled like the shimmering waters of Lake Barkley where the rocky island lingered as a "still" place in my memory.

The plane left the warm sunshine of North Carolina for the land with 10,000 lakes, and I was reminded of my ice-skating days in Canada a long time ago when snow sprayed the air as I skimmed over the frozen river.

Before I realized it, the plane was landing in Minneapolis where our old friend Bill Swanson swept me up in a bear hug. His wife Wilma was waiting at home for my arrival. She had a pot of coffee and some Jule kakke, and a desk in the corner for my writing. That "still" island comes in many forms. My "corner" looked out over snow-covered gardens.

That night Bill opened an old cedar chest. Handmade quilts and baby clothes came out. With them walked the memories of yesterday — the good and the difficult years of the past. We found ourselves harmonizing the old songs, especially, "Through it all, Through it all, I've learned to trust in Jesus . . ."

As Bill held up tiny baby shoes, we were reminded again that our children are walking through their valleys and mountains. Someday their cedar chest would be filled with memories. Our prayer was that they, too, would sing, "Through it all, Through it all, we've learned to trust in Jesus . . ."

Out came photo albums. Pictures of past generations brought to mind the words of the psalmist: "LORD, thou hast been our dwelling place in all generations" (Psalm 90:1).

One by one, each item was placed back into the chest. Bill closed the lid gently. There would be another time.

Alone in the bedroom, late into the night, I thought of life's cedar chest and the stored memories we can't part with. Then again, there are some memories we need to discard. I would be sharing some of the good memories with college students, business men and churches while I was a guest in the Swanson home.

There was a time when Mama's children opened the

chest of memories, then closed the lid on the "why" of yesterday and opened the door on the "how" of tomorrow.

Each one of Mama's children knew what atonement meant. Being at one with God through Jesus Christ affected every area of our lives. We had heard Papa preach and Mama pray. And we knew that when Jesus set His face to the cross He made it possible for us to walk *into* a new day *from* the cross. It was not enough for us to give a mental assent to Papa's teachings on the death and resurrection of Jesus Christ. It was not even enough for Mama to pray. The power of the Holy Spirit made us realize the redemptive work of God in our lives; and the Holy Spirit made the life of Christ in us visible in the marketplace. This we knew. This was the anchor, the absolute in our lives, from which we did not waver.

Oswald Chambers wrote: "The Holy Spirit is deity in processing power, who applies the atonement to our experience." All Mama and Papa's children came to understand the processing power of God as we opened our chest of memories and allowed God's indwelling presence to bring renewal to our minds.

In Ephesians 1:16-23, Paul prayed that our understanding would be enlightened that we might know the working of His power wrought in Christ Jesus. What a prayer!

When Jesus was leaving His disciples, He promised never to leave them alone. The Father would send the Comforter, the Holy Spirit, who would teach them all things and bring to remembrance what had been told them (John 14:26).

Looking back, I marvel at God's processing power to bring to remembrance the things stored in life's "cedar chest."

I lift the lid slowly, cautiously, looking in my heart for a picture showing the family gathered for Thanksgiving dinner in Brooklyn Church on 57th street.

Papa was closing the door on sixty-eight years of

preaching the gospel. Mama had prepared her last family Thanksgiving dinner. Together we helped with the packing in preparation for their retirement in Florida where they would be near Jeanelle, their youngest child.

All day Papa had packed his books in boxes — some to be given away, others to be sent to Florida. Mama lovingly marked her earthly treasures with her children's names.

It was late when we said, "Good night, Mama. Good night, Papa." He was still in his study, surrounded by boxes and empty shelves. When morning came, Mama's coffee pot sent the message, and the sleeping household came alive.

But Papa, his face grey with grief, was sitting in his study — where his books were back on the shelf. Gordon broke the silence. "Just leave the books, Papa, and I will send them to you when you get your study ready."

Mama urged gently, "Come, Papa, it is time for coffee."

Later Papa shuffled back to his books while Mama and her children continued packing. Papa was in his place.

I put that memory back in its place. From the "heart chest" I drew out another picture.

During one of Papa's earlier visits to our home, he sat playing the piano. His music stopped abruptly. "What's wrong, Papa?" I asked.

He shook his snow-white head. "Margaret, I just realized that I am seventy years old and I'll never play the piano any better than I play today. I always wanted to play well. And now the years have passed too fast. Too fast," he mumbled solemnly. "All my life I wanted to do everything better — to improve my English and my preaching. Ja, the time, it goes too fast."

He reached for his Bible, but he couldn't read. His eyes were filled with tears. I didn't know what to say, so

I put my arms around him and pressed my cheek against his. He didn't seem to notice — he just turned to his Book.

I put the picture back in my "chest" and wondered if I could have said more — and did he notice?

Thirteen years before, when Papa returned from Norway, he had made one of his rare visits to our home. He was vibrant, as happy as a little boy coming home from camp. We sat at the table drinking coffee and he recalled his visit to the old homeplace after forty years.

In glowing terms, Papa told about his beautiful sisters and their fine children. Knute, his older brother, a powerful, muscular man, lived alone on the Tweten farm in Bamble, Norway. Papa was proud of his family. We laughed when he told about Uncle Knute's straw bed. "Ja, Margaret, I burned Knute's straw bed and bought a real bed with a good mattress. Believe me, Knute wasn't happy about that, but I suggested to him that he should sleep in the new bed for one week."

Papa chuckled delightedly. "He never mentioned the straw bed again."

I listened to stories of bravery that came out of the nightmare of the Nazi occupation of Norway. The bunkers in the yards told the story of that tragic hour. But Knute, who lived alone in a remote area, had escaped German occupation of his home.

Papa sent frantic requests to Mama in America for coffee, linens, curtains and even medication that was unattainable in Norway at that time. That morning as we sat at the kitchen table, I saw a practical side of Papa as he told of making repairs on the old family home and painting the house and barn. Joy and nostalgia blended as he told about getting new appliances into the old kitchen, even a radio. Knute, the recluse, got a view of the world through the eyes of his younger brother.

During his evenings in Norway, Papa sang and played his guitar and read the Bible to Knute. Uncle Knute gave

Papa a black horse called Midnight. During the visit, Midnight and Papa were inseparable. I had visions of Papa riding in the valley through snow-covered woods. He told of sleigh rides and falling into snow banks, of green pastures and spring, of birds and flowers, hills and mountains.

Every day Knute carried his lunch pail into the forest where he cut lumber for his livelihood. The two brothers, so different, were one in the old homeplace where once rang the laughter of father, mother, sisters and brothers.

Papa sang the old songs while his older brother listened pensively about another world he would never see — America.

I had a picture in my heart of Uncle Knute sitting on the porch looking out over the fields and woods as the sun cast a glow over his world. He would never understand what a man could learn from books in a musty library, in America. Here in Bamble, a man walked tall like the towering timber of the woods. Grain from the fields and food from the gardens filled the barns. Besides that, hunting and fishing provided all a man needed. In the evening, a quiet contentment filled Knute's heart. What could a man find in books that he — Knute Tweten — didn't have? He had the majesty of mountains, waterfalls and crystal springs, animals for company, birds to sing in the early morning and the song of doves in the evening time. Knute was content.

If there were the mystery of a woman's love in Uncle Knute's life, the secret lay buried within him. He communed only with God and His creation around him. Uncle Knute was in his place.

But Papa, the younger brother lost in his books, was also in his place.

I closed the lid softly. There would be another time to look into memory's cedar chest.

14

The Winds of March, 1973

IN MARCH OF 1973, Papa's children were gathered around the fireplace singing, "Surely goodness and mercy shall follow me all the days, all the days of my life . . ."

Mama, her frail hands folded, rocked quietly and sang with us.

Across the road from Doris and David's home in North Carolina, the wind blew over a fresh, lonely grave. Near their place, a yellow house stood watch over the valley — the dream house where Mama and Papa had planned to live. Inside, the study was full of Papa's books, a study he would never see.

Papa had gone Home!

Mama would make that final move from Florida into the yellow house in North Carolina alone — yet, not alone, for goodness and mercy would follow her.

My heart was tender as I heard Harold's words over Papa's grave, "Lord, Thou hast been our dwelling place to all generations. Thou art God. Lord, in Elius N. Tweten — Papa to all of us — was a man in whom was no guile. A man who trusted God, stood up for Jesus and believed and defended the Bible as God's divinely inspired Word . . . 'Blessed are the pure in heart.' "

Harold concluded with Papa's familiar benediction:

Now the God of peace,
that brought again from the dead our Lord Jesus,
that great shepherd of the sheep,
through the blood of the everlasting covenant,
make you perfect in every good work to do His will,
working in you that which is well-pleasing in His sight,
through Jesus Christ;
to whom be glory for ever and ever. Amen.
(Hebrews 13:20,21)

Papa had served the God of peace for many years. Now the man who had struggled with anger as his one prevailing flaw had been made perfect. We couldn't grieve, for somehow in our imagination we saw Papa in the libraries of heaven talking with his beloved authors, Charles Haddon Spurgeon and Matthew Henry. From out of the past came the lawgiver Moses, the prophet Isaiah, the poet David, philosophers, teachers and preachers. The living Book was now alive to Papa. He left his books to meet the authors, particularly the Author and Finisher of his faith.

Papa was in his place.

One by one, Mama's children took the journey into the past with its mountains and valleys, sunshine and shadow, agony and ecstasy. Each of Mama's children came through to view the yesterdays with love and understanding, instead of judgment and condemnation.

The great Communicator, the Holy Spirit, had built a bridge from the minister in the pulpit to the father who had broken communication with his family because of one tragic sin — uncontrolled anger.

The very Word that Papa preached — James 1:19 — warns us all to be slow to anger. Anger and wisdom seldom live together. Somewhere along life's way I had heard that "anger is a wind which blows out the lamp of the mind." With the passing of years, Mama's children could open the chest of memories and discard the wood, hay and stubble and remember the gold and silver of Papa's life.

We discarded the memories of how we all desired to take Mama out of the "winds of anger" and carry her to our "safe" places. Instead, we kept the covenant God had with Mama. Mama would trust and obey. God would keep her children by His power. Mama did not fail — God could not fail. We kept the gold and silver, knowing that the Lord was a strong tower; the righteous could run there and be safe.

Together we discarded the winds of anger directed at us in our youth when "Papa's reason and wisdom's lamp went out." Together we kept the gold that came on the wings of love and understanding. The great Communicator kept building bridges for us.

Over the years, Mama had listened quietly while her children opened the lid on yesterday and watched as the balm of Gilead, the matchless love of God, the comfort of the Holy Spirit, brought healing to her wounded children. She knew. God could not fail.

Grace, the quiet peacemaker, had always typed Papa's sermons and helped him with his correspondence. Like David of old who soothed Saul's restless spirit, Grace played the music that was the one major area of communication between Papa and the children.

From the dark and dusty backroads of the mind,

Grace discarded the stubble and remembered the gold — the trips with Papa to the great Moody Memorial Church to hear outstanding Bible teachers, the concerts in Radio City and the visits to Calvary Baptist Church in New York. Papa was unashamedly proud of Grace's accomplishments, especially her work in Switzerland with the Billy Graham Conference. Before his death, the time did come — suddenly, like a flash of lightning — when Papa saw us as adults and expressed his delight in Mama's children. "Ja, ja, Mama, you did a good job!"

Joyce Solveig, who had cringed in fear during the winds of Papa's anger, was now remembering a childhood moment in his loving arms. It was during a 17th-of-May festival in Humboldt Park, Chicago. In the excitement of the Norwegian parade, Joyce wandered away into the crowd.

Over the noise of the crowd came the booming voice on the loud speaker, "Will Reverend Tweten please come to 'Lost and Found' to get his daughter?"

Joyce shuddered. Knowing how angry Papa would be was worse than being lost. She saw him stride through the crowd, pushing his way free. The anger didn't come.

Instead Joyce was swooped up in loving arms and held tenderly as he cried, "Min lilla Solveig, Min lilla Solveig (my little Solveig)."

"I remember feeling so safe and loved," Joyce whispered. "I wanted the moment to last forever."

Today, Joyce has discarded the fear of Papa and kept the gold of "safe and loved" in her memory chest.

Doris walked with Gordon through the winds of anger, gently leading him to unconditional love and forgiveness. They discarded the chaff and stubble from the storehouse of yesterday. For Gordon there was inner peace from the bitter memory of a shiny fifty-cent piece rolling across the floor. Together — as Doris and Gordon thought of Papa — they clung to the gold and silver of unconditional love and forgiveness.

Peace had come for Gordon long before Papa's death, and with tears of joy, the beautiful reconciliation between father and son was fully realized through the power of the Holy Spirit. On that grand occasion, they had faced one another at the table — two stubborn, independent men — weeping, hugging, forgiving, loving. The love of God was shed abroad in the hearts of all of Mama's children, and they chose to live in obedience to God. God would keep their children — and their children's children, from generation to generation.

Doris and I attended the James Mason prayer meeting on Tuesday nights where we saw the miracles of God's so great salvation — and the salvation of my son, Ralph.

This godly, white-haired man, James Mason, had become the spiritual father we never knew. From him we learned that love never fails. We learned to discard the "why" of yesterday and to turn to the "how" for tomorrow. Paul and Silas hadn't cried "why" and like them Mr. Mason moved on to the "how" — singing praises to the God of his salvation.

One night, two years before Papa's death, Doris and I took Papa to hear Mr. Mason. Music burst forth from the piano, organ and other instruments, blending with the voices of praise of the people in the room. These people had been set free from the bondage of the past and were singing songs that the world could not understand. It was the sweet sound of "Amazing Grace."

Papa listened. He heard the same message he had preached, yet he sensed a spirit of love and praise that was deeper than he had ever known.

Late that night, he looked at me with misty eyes. "Tell me, Margaret. Did I miss something? In all my years of preaching, did I miss something?"

He was eighty-three years old, still ramrod straight. I answered gently, "Papa, you have faithfully preached God's Word all these years according to the light you had."

"Ja, ja, Margaret, I have been faithful." He ran his

hand through his snow-white hair. "That I know, but Mr. Mason has something — a love — that I have missed."

Inside, I wanted to cry out, *You did miss it, Papa! You missed the love and communication with your children. You missed walking gently with Mama.* I almost choked, thinking, *you missed the worth of your son Gordon. You missed the victory over the sin of anger.* I could have lashed out at him so easily saying, *You never realized that the power of God in you was greater than the anger that came from the enemy. Satan wanted to destroy you, Papa. But the enemy didn't win — for you were kept by the power of God. You were kept by the same power that raised Jesus from the dead and was able to make you more than a conqueror over the winds of anger. You did miss a lot of things — but you didn't miss God's unchanging love!*

I wanted to cry it out — tell him at last — but after all these years, I couldn't say it. Papa stood before me, his white hair framing his sad, tear-filled eyes. I could only put my arms around him.

Tonight, two years later, Jeanelle remembers the outpouring of his heart before God took our father home.

It was as though the Holy Spirit, the great Communicator, had brought to his memory all he had missed. Then like sunrise after a long dark night, God let Papa hear the song of the soul set free: "Amazing grace! how sweet the sound . . ."

Once again Mama's children looked into the chest of memories and piece by piece we put the gold and silver back into the treasure chest.

With Gordon, we sang together, "Oh, come, let us adore Him . . . For Thou alone art worthy, Christ — The Lord."

Oh, so gently we closed the lid. Jesus had spoken "Peace, be still!" to the winds of anger.

15

The Blizzard

TOMORROW THE PLANE WILL TAKE ME back to the sunshine of Wilmington, North Carolina. Today, in Bloomington, Minnesota, 1986, I watch the snow swirling outside, beyond the reach of my cozy corner where I write. From my window I see the blanket of snow that covers the brown grass of fall. Naked, barren tree limbs stretch toward the soft snow flurries that are already hiding their leafless branches. The world all around me is dressed in a coat of diamond-studded white ermine.

Last night I told the stories of my childhood memories of Christmas in Canada to an audience in the beautiful Blue Room of Northwestern College in St Paul, Minnesota.

A mellow tenor led us in singing, "I'm dreaming of a white Christmas." I'll remember that song when I get back to North Carolina. The tenor and I laughed together

over the Christmas traditions of lute fisk and rice pudding.
I admitted, "It is a shame for a good Norwegian like me
to dislike lute fisk — but I can't stand that slippery fish!"

I took the audience back to the Canada of 1920 and
told them how Papa welcomed the lonely immigrants at
the train station in Winnipeg and invited them home for
a Norwegian Christmas Eve — with lute fisk!

Following the festive meal, we marched around the
Christmas tree singing the carols in Norwegian and English.
While singing, Johnny and Bjarne stumbled into the parsonage after walking eighty miles in the freezing Canadian
winter.

I told them about Papa becoming a missionary to the
Scandinavian settlers in the province of Saskatchewan.
They listened intently to the story of the Tweten trek from
Winnipeg to Saskatoon where we encountered an Oriental
man and a small restaurant in an open field.

Papa stopped to get a cup of coffee or a 5-cent bowl
of soup for Mama. We were warned that there was no
money so we had to be content with homemade bread
and some water.

With a smile, the Oriental man kept urging us to
come into his restaurant. Papa protested, "We have no
money." The smiling man insisted. He led us to a table
with a white linen cloth, and then he prepared dinner for
us all. My vivid memory was that of Mama being served.
It was our first experience in a restaurant.

After a delicious dinner, we all shook hands and said,
"Takk for matten [Thank you for the food]." Papa promised
to return someday to pay the man for his kindness, then
we were on our way.

After we were settled in our four-room yellow house,
Papa returned to repay the man for his kindness. There
was no restaurant. The neighbors assured Papa there had
never been an Oriental living in the vicinity. Puzzled
beyond understanding, Papa went back for Mama.

"Ja, Papa, I know exactly where the place is and I

will show you," she told him. But there was only a breeze blowing gently over the empty field.

Years later, Papa told the story to Jeanelle. "No one would have believed it so we never mentioned it, but now I am convinced we saw an angel." God had sent an Oriental man with a smiling face to feed the Twetens.

Now it was Christmas in Saskatoon, where the happy festivities of Winnipeg were only memories. In the four-room house, with an outhouse at the end of a path, we faced the stark reality of another threadbare Christmas. A lonely tree with handmade decorations stood in the corner but there were no gifts — not only no gifts, but no food and no Papa.

Papa was on a missionary journey in the northern part of Canada. Mama deliberately set the table for Christmas.

"But, Mama, will we have Christmas?" I asked.

"Ja, we have Christmas, Margaret. God will provide. He never fails. We are warm and we have oatmeal and bread — even coffee and sugar lumps. Christmas? Of course we have Christmas." Her lovely face shone as bright as the Christmas star. "We have Jesus in our hearts. That is Christmas!"

"But Mama, we always have presents."

"We have God's gift to us. See, we have the table set for Christmas. We have the tree. We have our songs and stories — and you ask, 'Will we have Christmas?' We have *Christ-mas!* Come — a bath now, and then a nap. Then we dress for Christmas Eve." She jabbed at the big-bone hair pin that held her figure-eight bun in place.

"Where is Papa?" I asked.

She paused, her slender hands on her hips. "God knows where Papa is." Mama answered. Her hands fell limp against the crisp starched apron that covered her plain, dark dress. She smiled to reassure me. "A bath — come, we get the tub."

The round metal tub was for Saturday night baths when everyone got ready for Sunday. The only exception was the Christmas Eve bath — in the middle of the week.

After the scrub in the tub we were clothed in the new long underwear that Mama made for Christmas Eve. Then to bed for a nap — a ritual no one dared to break. "Sleep now!" Mama said.

We did! We dreamed of Christmas dinner, lots of people, singing and marching around the tree. Always, there was one present each. Tonight, only oatmeal — and no presents. But Mama said we would have Christmas. God and Mama never failed.

The house was still. Mama put on the coffee pot.

Soon the house was stirring and Mama dressed her four children for Christmas. I was proud, proud of the bright hair bow perched on my head. This was the night of nights — Christmas Eve.

Mama gathered us around her rocking chair and told the story of angels and shepherds, wise men and gifts, but the greatest part of all was the baby in the straw. We sang the songs of Christmas and I looked longingly at the lonely tree in the corner.

Suddenly the sound of stomping feet filled the winter night. Mama opened the door to a group of happy young people and their pastor, Dr. Ward. He was grinning when he said, "We heard that the Norwegian missionary had not returned from his journey and since this is your first Christmas in Saskatoon, we thought you might enjoy a special Christmas from your Canadian friends."

With shouts of laughter, the young people placed gifts under the tree and put a prepared dinner on the prepared table. Candy, fruit and nuts were added to the bountiful supply.

Together we sang the carols of Christmas and once again the story was read of God's gift to man. A closing prayer followed the invitation to have Christmas dinner at the home of Dr. Ward, pastor of the Baptist church of Saskatoon. I was delighted! We always had the lonely people to our house and now we were invited out as "company."

Their retreating steps echoed in the snow. Mama's face was shining. Her faith had been rewarded. *She had known we would have Christmas!*

We rushed into action — the butter, salt and pepper, water in the glasses, roast chicken, even cranberry sauce — there was no end to delicacies — cookies, fruit cake. But best of all, no lute fisk!

Then we heard another sound of crunching footsteps in the snow — just outside the door. The door burst open and there stood Papa! His place was already set at the table. "Faith and works go together," Mama said.

Papa rubbed his cold hands to warm them. "I was lost in a blizzard — but now I am home — safe and warm," he said.

The joy of Christmas filled the house with laughter and songs. Faith filled my heart. Late into the night, we listened to Papa's story of how he was lost in a blizzard.

His eyes sparkled. "The snow swirled around me in blinding fury while the wind beat against me. I was all alone, lost in a world of white. I stood still — then I cried to the Lord. 'God, I am lost, but You aren't lost. You know where I am. Please guide me to a safe place.' "

With awe in his voice, Papa told how a warm Presence drew close and he followed the warmth to a cabin nearly covered by snow. There he stayed and helped the pioneer family shovel a path to the barn. He helped milk the cow, gather eggs, and cut wood for the stove. The family and Papa cared for each other until the storm passed.

I paused for a moment as I looked over my audience — handsome business men and their beautifully dressed wives. The room glowed with candlelight, the people sipped cranberry punch. Then I continued. "During the winter storms in Colorado when my husband Harold was a boy, his mother warned, 'Don't cut across the open fields but follow the fence along the road to school.'

"Harold and the other children trudged to school through the high snow drifts, staying close to the fence all the way. No one dared to blaze a short cut through the open fields." I leaned forward, closer to my audience. "We face many blizzards in life — broken relationships, broken dreams, losses and tragedy. Life's blizzards come and we feel trapped by the storms swirling around us."

The smartly dressed business man directly in front of me twirled his glass of cranberry punch. I watched him as I said, "My father cried out to God, 'I'm lost.' "

The man looked up and nodded. My gaze swept across the room to other faces. "Jesus speaks to us across the storms of life and warns, 'Don't take a short cut across the fields of man's philosophy. Stay close to the fence — the marker — the way.' For remember, Jesus said, 'I am the way!' "

I paused, looking at the flickering candles on the tables. There was a warm glow in my heart when I told them, "Out of the past I seem to hear Papa say, 'I was lost, but God brought me home . . . not only home to Mama and the children on Christmas Eve — but home to God.' "

16

Songs in the Night

IT WAS 1975 WHEN MAMA AND HER DAUGHTERS stood beside the second grave on the hill. The wind cried in the valley as another sound echoed from the courts of heaven — the sound of a soul set free. Our brother, Gordon, had been cut down in the prime of his life with an aneurysm. The reunion between father and son was now complete. Through our heartache and tears, we joined in singing, "Amazing grace! how sweet the sound . . ."

Like Papa, Gordon had a restless nature, an unquenchable thirst for knowledge and a bent toward independence. He was an intellectual man — a man who could be both cynical and compassionate, stubborn and gentle. He was a good friend, a hard worker, a man given to laughter — and a man consumed with goals. Gordon had an unending love for books and music, New York City, and his wife and children. He was also Mama's "boy" and a brother adored by his sisters. But for years a distance existed between Papa and Gordon — father and son. Finally the seeds of faith that had been planted in Gordon in childhood — and had always been part of him — burst forth in his adulthood. He became a spiritual giant — a man who experienced and extended unconditional love and forgiveness. Gordon became what he had always been deep inside — a man with a warm, responsive heart.

If God had given us the choice, we would have said, "It's too soon, Lord. He's too young." But deep within we knew that Gordon was free — at home with his Savior and walking the courts of heaven with Papa. We could not ask for more.

> Gordon Lund Tweten
> The sound of taps across the hill,
> A silent pause,
> And the world is still.
> A swaying branch of scented pine,
> Gentle breezes
> Over the hills of time.
> Light fills the glory of the dawn,
> Eternal Home!
> Glorious sunrise — earth's shadows gone!
> Worship and praise around the throne,
> Hallelujahs ring,
> Worthy, worthy, worthy is my King.

"The blanket of snow covers the bleakness of winter," Mama had always said, "but when winter comes, the next thing to come is spring." Just so, the blanket of God's love covers the bleakness of sad memories. Mama had only a year and a half — just one springtime left — after Gordon's homegoing.

On January 16, 1977, at 2 P.M. — with a blanket of snow outside covering the bleakness of winter — we gathered to say good-bye to Mama. The quiet memorial service defied the blizzard raging on the other side of the church walls. "Let not your heart be troubled" once again sounded across the pages of time.

A settled faith lingered in the hearts of the five sisters, Mama's daughters. We followed her grey casket into the icy wind — so reminiscent of the Canadian winters.

We buried Mama beside Papa and Gordon. The two older graves were covered with snow. Bundled in coats and scarves, we braced ourselves against the wind and huddled together around Mama's open grave.

Across the road Mama's yellow house stood empty and silent, the coffee pot cold.

Slowly we walked to Doris and David's big house where logs blazed with warmth and the coffee was hot. An amber glow of love engulfed us. We knew that Mama was safe in the house of the Lord forever. The restless stream, Papa, and the flowing river, Mama, were eternally united by God's amazing grace.

Papa, Mama and Gordon — all in their place.

The winter of the soul will pass. The next thing to come is spring for "some golden daybreak, Jesus will come!" Then we shall see Him face to face.

> Dear Lord,
> "Please take our reservation.
> Mark down the time and place
> Where we may walk together
> And talk face to face.
> We know there will be many
> Singing of Your grace,
> But — take our reservation.
> Mark down our time and place."
> — Margaret, Grace, Doris, Joyce Solveig, Jeanelle.

17

Papa's Bible

I AM HOME AGAIN where the sun shines on the pampas grass and the ocean rolls over the sandy shore. The Minnesota snow is a fading memory. But the love and warmth of friends stay gently on my mind.

This morning my "still" place is the kitchen with my books and yellow legal pages strewn over the table. It is early and the world is asleep, but my coffee pot is awake.

In my hands I hold two books. One is my father's Norwegian Bible; the other, his Norwegian song book, *Evangelisten*. The note in the Bible says:

Dear Margaret,
    This is for you, in loving memory of your father.
                                        Love, Mother, 1973.

Turning the yellow pages of the song book, I read

the words of the familiar lullaby that I used with our children. Now I sing the same song to my grandchildren:

"Sangen om Jesus

Syng den igjen, igjen.

(Songs about Jesus, sing them again and again)."

Sermon notes are tucked between the pages of the Bible and song book. Some are written in Norwegian, others in English. My childhood language returns with the help of a Norwegian dictionary as I look at one of Papa's sermons on the "Grace of God and Reasons to Believe." The sermon closes with Romans 11:33: "O the depth of the riches both of the wisdom and knowledge of God! How unsearchable are his judgments, and his ways past finding out!"

I reach for the books on my shelf — Papa's worn treasury of David. (It has taken me four years to get to Spurgeon's fourth volume.)

The marked pages in Spurgeon's read, "The Bible should be our Mentor, Monitor, our Memento Mori, our Remembrance and the keeper of our conscience."

My sister Joyce Solveig has a favorite picture of Papa, with his snow-white head bent over the open Bible. My mental picture is one of Papa meticulously dressed in his striped trousers, swallow tail coat and high starched collar. (Mama alone ironed Papa's starched shirt for Sundays.)

When Papa stood behind the pulpit and opened his Bible, it was with a sense of awe that Mama and her children knew that Papa was in his place. To Papa, the pulpit was the sacred place from which mortal man proclaimed, "Thus saith the Lord."

It is through this memory that Mama's children are able to leave the quicksand of human speculation as to the why of Papa's winds of anger. From this we are able to move to the higher ground of God's divine love and matchless grace.

To all of us who have been wounded by winds of

anger, in whatever form the storms come, there is only one place of surety — the cross. "The cross," according to Oswald Chambers, "is the point where God and sinful man merge with a crash, and the way to life is opened — but the crash is on the heart of God." Only at the cross can we realize how much we have been forgiven; then we can cry out, "I forgive as I have been forgiven."

In Harry Dent's book *Cover Up* he deals with the Watergate in all of us, the desire to cover up. For me, it would have been easy to cover the winds of anger, but in my travel, I have heard the cries of many who have been wounded by life's storms. The storms of anger can damage all of us, but the stagnant pool of *unforgiveness* will *destroy us.*

Only when we are uncovered to the grace of God can we be covered by the love of God. There is no firmer ground than "forgiveness."

All through the pages of Papa's sermons I read the message of God's grace and mercy — and "God is faithful." Today I finally see Papa as a man hungry for God, the way God must have seen him. Yesterday, I saw only the storm in the man.

Through the ages God's perfect plan has been carried out through imperfect people. Looking through the notes, I smiled at Papa's three-point sermons. One caught my attention:

A Formula for Duty Living:
    1. Prayer — Motivating force.
    2. Pluck — Impelling force.
    3. Perspiration — Accomplishing force.

I think back, remembering the day when Papa took me to Paul Rader's tabernacle in Chicago to hear Gypsy Smith.

"Listen to Gypsy Smith's words, Margaret," Papa told me. "He paints pictures with words like an artist paints with oil. Every time I hear Gypsy Smith he makes the gospel fresh and new. Margaret, we must never lose the wonder of the cross."

I read from the marked Spurgeon volume: "It is not enough to read the Bible. Meditation assists the memory to lock up the jewels of divine truth in her treasury. It has the digesting power to turn special truth into nourishment. It helps to renew the heart to grow upward and increase in power to know the things freely given of God."

Again I am reminded that we must act upon truth or it becomes dry rot within us.

While I was sorting through Papa's papers, the phone rang. It was Monroe Holvick, an old friend of the family. After their fifty-one years of a happy marriage, his wife Leona had died at the age of ninety-two. Monroe was remembering their years as rural American Sunday school missionaries.

"I was led to the Lord in your father's church," Monroe choked, "and your father baptized me and married Leona and me."

Moments later he said, "Leona and I read *First We Have Coffee* three times and we laughed and cried together, remembering many happy hours in your home."

"Monroe, tell me, what do you remember the most about my father? I'm writing a sequel to *First We Have Coffee*, a book called *Papa's Place.*"

"Oh, how wonderful! Your father? The Bible, Margaret. He was a man with the BOOK. How he loved the Word of God!"

"Did you remember his explosive temper?"

A quiet pause followed, then gently Monroe answered, "I loved him too much to remember that part. I only remember how much your Papa loved God and people in need. Every time he preached, we went home with something to remember."

Kindly he added, "Even Moses had a temper, Margaret."

When our conversation ended, I realized again how much love covers and I prayed, "Lord, help me to see others through eyes of love, rather than judgment."

I reach into Papa's sermon notes again and see this:

Amazing Love:
1. Nature.
2. Object.
3. Gift.
4. Blessing.
5. Terms laid down by God.

How Papa loved oratory! He practiced for hours to improve his English. His notes to himself read:

1. Don't argue — persuade.
2. Move toward a decision.
3. Have a key sentence.
4. Phrase with care — phrase simply.

The more I read, the more I realize what a great teacher he would have been. From my perspective now, I can visualize him in a classroom — fulfilling his lifelong dream — teaching all that was stored up inside of him.

In one of his wistful moods, I recall how Papa told me that he had a secret dream to go to a great university and get his doctor's degree in theology. But someone had suggested that he was needed to minister to the Scandinavian people. The dream was buried.

Was he thinking of that dream as he prepared for his ordination? He had written: "Man comes to a sense of his own greatness only after he has humbled himself in the dust before the majesty of God. God does not want man to obey out of fear and cringe before Him. He wants man to stand up, a new creation in Christ, and God can speak to him. Man must stand erect, girt and ready to obey. There is no room for pride, since we are not our own. All power is given."

Perfection was important to Papa. I recall how angry

he became when we didn't enunciate words properly. "Speak up! Stand up straight! Look people in the eye when you shake hands!" he told us.

Now I can smile, but it wasn't humorous at the time.

"Go polish your shoes! Brush your hair! Don't disgrace the ministry!" It was always "the ministry."

I continue reading from Papa's notes: "People can only be induced willingly to do what they want to do. A good speaker clears the mind of the audience from previous thoughts; then the hearer can be introduced to your message."

When I turn the page, I read:

1. How do you go on when no one is listening?

2. Why am I sent to work where circumstances are adverse?

3. Am I merely a man exposed to conflict, pain and failure?

Papa answered his own questions, saying, "The answer is that life is a campaign, not a holiday. We go on because a prophet is sent by God with a message. It is in the battle where we prove our mettle."

At this point I stop to ask myself the questions, Do I really listen? Do I wait to hear from God before I speak? Do I hear what people really say, or do I hear words? And then I pray, "Spirit of the living God, fall fresh on me."

In the morning stillness I turn to Psalm 18 where David remembers the blessings of the Lord. Spurgeon suggests that, like David of old, we should publish abroad the story of the covenant of the cross, the Father's election, the Son's redemption and the Spirit's regeneration. Write a memorial of God's mercies he says, not only for our comfort, but for our children and grandchildren. Then our children will also rejoice in the Lord. In the margin I wrote: "Take heart, Margaret, and write (May 1982)."

Somehow it seems that I am discovering Papa's depth, touching his soul as I read his sermon notes.

Sins of Civilization:
1. Spiritual ingratitude.
2. Moral corruption.
3. Spiritual pride.
4. Ecclesiastical complacency.

Beside the four points, he had written: "There can be no religion where human rights are not recognized. The day of Jehovah is a day of searching — judgment. We could change human lives by persuading them to believe that by the grace of God their lives could be changed."

Over and over Papa wrote his sermon points, asked heart-searching questions and wrote his answers.

Knowledge of God Gained From:
1. Notice.
2. Scripture.
3. Observation.
4. Experience.

"Son of man," Papa wrote, "stand upon your feet! *Why?* 1. God asks you to. 2. You are a man — erect. 3. God wants to speak to you. 4. So — listen. 5. Look. 6. Go. 7. Prove yourself a man."

Great expository preachers inspired Papa, men like G. Campbell Morgan. According to *A School of Christ* by Nathan Wood, Morgan's weekly convocation lectures at Gordon College, Wenham, Massachusetts, in 1920-1931 are remembered as some of his greatest work. Morgan left a lasting impression on eight generations of Gordon students. He brought an example of expository preaching with vivid phrasing, logic and diction and a voice ranging from confidential whispers to deep, organ-like tones.

Dr. Harry A. Ironside, another man that Papa admired, completed the exposition of the entire Bible during his seventeen years as pastor of the great Moody Memorial Church in Chicago.

Perhaps because Papa never reached his own theological goals, he wanted us to hear great preaching from outstanding men of God like Dr. R. A. Torrey, Dr. Harry A. Ironsides, Dr. Will Houghton and Dr. V. Raymond Edmman. Papa greatly admired Dr. Scarborough and Dr. R. G. Lee from the South and Dr. William Ward Ayer, the pastor of New York City's Calvary Baptist Church.

When the young men came on the scene, Papa rejoiced to see the great evangelistic emphasis by Dr. Torrey Johnson, founder of Youth for Christ; Dr. Robert Cook, President of King's College; and Billy Graham.

During Billy Graham's first New York Crusade, Papa was deeply moved. Later he told me, "I found myself weeping as I watched humanity coming like mountain streams from the balcony and moving toward the river of life. Margaret, I'll never forget what I saw — with my own eyes. The simple message of the gospel is still the power of God to change lives."

As I read Papa's notes, I see his struggles and convictions. "When the hearer in the pew hears from the pulpit 'Thus saith the Lord,' he has a choice to make. Either the hearer chooses to obey or he chooses to disobey."

Again he wrote: "Obedience to truth is the simple way. Most of us know what to do, but would rather spend hours discussing the why of the situation, rather than obey God's *how* to move to higher spiritual ground. So simple — just not easy."

Mama's quiet walk of obedience brought a steadying factor into a household's encounter with "storms." God had His own way of weaving a tapestry of "all things" for good.

When I recall bits and pieces of conversation with Papa, I can now sense his frustration at being ahead of his time. He was hemmed into one sphere of service when his outlook was ecumenical. He longed for the fellowship of all believers in Christ, longed to escape being bound by diverse doctrinal barriers.

Today I see the crumbling of the divisive wall and I rejoice in the fellowship of "oneness in Christ Jesus."

How Papa would rejoice to see me tell the old story of Jesus and His love to a Catholic audience, and then share the same message in a Baptist church.

In a formal setting of robes and candles, I tell the simplicity of "God so loved the world," and we kneel together. In the informal setting of drums and guitars, we also praise the Lord together.

Someone once came to me and said, "You are doing all the things that were in your father's heart to do." (Thank You, Lord!)

Then there was the night when 7,000 people at the Booksellers Convention gathered in Kennedy Center to praise God. When we stood together, representing all denominations, and sang the Hallelujah Chorus, I thought the heavens would open. (Didn't I hear Papa shouting all over God's heaven?)

I close Papa's Bible and put his journal notes and song book away. I have just had a fresh glimpse of Papa — a glimpse of his own searching heart — a glimpse that poured a fresh healing balm on my own memories. I sense his frustrations, his insatiable quest for books, his unfinished theological dreams and goals.

I had seen Papa stretching tiptoe toward his God and I had seen him silently weeping, struggling with his winds of anger. A proud man. A godly man.

From his journals, I knew him with a new intensity. How much Papa had loved God and Mama and his children. Again I realized that Papa had bypassed his own childhood. He was a boy grown up too soon — a young man thrust into responsibility before his time. Papa had suffered great losses as a child — his siblings, his parents. At seventeen, he had struck out alone for America.

In Mama and in his God Papa had found strength and sure-footing. In his books and in his preaching he had found acceptance. One thing I knew as I closed his journals — something I had always known — Papa loved his children. Perhaps he left the rearing of the children

to Mama in order to keep a safe distance, to veil his fear
of losing us as he had lost his siblings and my younger
sister, Bernice. From his children he had sought perfection,
demanded it. But from his journals I knew that Papa,
too, had sought to be God's perfect man.

Somehow it seems that Papa must be looking over
my shoulder, saying, "Ja, ja, Margaret, so you are reading
my notes?" I can almost hear him chuckle. "Ja, now
maybe you will listen."

Then again I can almost see him with a tear in his
eye. "Someday, Margaret, we'll talk it over. It is good to
write the joy and sorrow of life. But above all else, write
about God's grace and mercy."

18

The Road Home

ON OCTOBER 2, 1986, AT 7 P.M., my husband, my daughter and I settled back in our seats, fastened our seat belts, and prepared for take-off from the Boston airport: final destination — Papa's homeplace.

We were on our way! But the first stop would be Frankfurt, Germany, to attend the International Book Fair.

It was like a dream. Janice, Harold and I were drinking coffee on the Lufthansa Airline, while efficient flight attendants passed out delicious German pastries. Now there was time to relax and laugh at our mad scramble to get ready. Delayed passports, the air flight from North Carolina, and too much baggage all were a part of our departure.

Janice, our expert travel agent, had made all the arrangements — planes, trains and hotels. I settled back for a long nap.

As dawn came up over the ocean, we landed in the German airport of Frankfurt. A babble of strange voices and sounds surrounded us. It was then I knew how Papa felt when he landed at Ellis Island when he was only seventeen.

In the crowd, we spotted Linda and John Crone from Here's Life Publishers. They were waiting with flowers and a camera. John's camera flashed, catching our look of bewilderment on film — then, snapping our joy of recognition.

With people and baggage crammed into the car, John wended his way through traffic to a quaint village where the guest house looked like a picture post card. Lace curtains and window boxes with flowers looked out over a courtyard of gardens.

The cheerful rooms, and their feather beds, offered a welcome rest after the all-night flight.

The International Book Fair consisted of seven vast buildings of beautiful marble, glass and tile. Publishers from around the world displayed their latest publications in decorated booths. We were only three of the two hundred thousand visitors passing through the buildings that day.

Buildings with books! How Papa would have enjoyed the Book Fair. The religious publishers had their booths in a separate building. It was in this building that Here's Life Publishers had their display. As we passed the various booths, we heard a number of different languages but the message was always the same.

The Germans hosted a beautiful banquet for the evangelical publishers. As director of Women's Ministry in Grace Chapel, Lexington, Massachusetts, Janice believed that women's vision of the world could be enlarged through the exchange of ideas from world wide publishers.

At the close of the Sunday morning worship service, we stood to offer the Lord's prayer — each one in his own language.

Reluctantly, we said good-bye to Linda and John and

the beautiful city of Frankfurt, and we boarded a train for the twelve-hour ride to Copenhagen, Denmark.

When we arrived, and were settled in the hotel, we contacted Harold's family and took a cab to the home of Bodil Krogh, his gracious eighty-four-year-old cousin. Her white hair framed a delicate face with laughing blue eyes — a perfect reminder of Harold's beautiful mother.

Bodil opened an album that held a record of her American family. Later, at her only son's home, we sat at a table set with exquisite Copenhagen china, along with flowers and candles. Small American and Danish flags decorated each place setting. We joined hands and Harold prayed God's blessing on his Danish family. We left with tears of joy, knowing that we would meet again.

Before boarding the train for Stockholm, Sweden — our next stop en route to Papa's place — we arranged a tour of the beautiful city of Copenhagen which included seeing the Little Mermaid, the changing of the guard at the palace, a walk down the famous "walking street," where shoppers walk bumper to bumper, and the renowned Copenhagen Circus.

In Sweden, we spent the night at the Royal Viking with its crystal staircase. High tea at four o'clock included magnificent music by a lovely young harpist and tea with delicacies served by Swedish girls who spoke fluent English.

We were walking in a new world. Even the European breakfast was a delight with its boiled eggs, rolls, dark bread and platters artistically arranged with assorted cheese, ham and fish, served with strong coffee and rich cream.

The European trains, the hotels, the restaurants, shopping and civic events, the Stockholm symphony — we walked to them all, crowding them all in.

Finally with growing anticipation, we boarded the train for Oslo, Norway, where Bjorne and Rut Langmo met us and opened their lovely home to us. We went everywhere together — to the historic places, the beautiful parks and the monuments. In Oslo, people walked everywhere. Bicycles and baby buggies filled the walkways. Laughing children in bright wool hand-knit sweaters and caps were like a painting in perpetual motion. Sedate dogs walked beside their owners. The weather was like a New England autumn. Bands played in the parks. Guitars were strummed on the streets.

The most memorable monument was the Resistance Building, the historical museum that honored the bravery of the Norwegian Freedom Fighters and the people of Norway during the Nazi occupation. Monuments of Franklin D. Roosevelt and Winston Churchill were at the entrance. "Never Again" was the theme. I was proud to be an American and proud to be a part of these Norwegian people.

The churches were beautiful — but empty. Too many Europeans felt indifferent to their spiritual needs. Their fear of nuclear war was greater than their fear of eternity without God.

Bjorne and Rut took us to the Philadelphia Church in Oslo where we heard the Swedish chorus from Stockholm. What music! The young people from the Philadelphia Church go out, with their guitars, into the streets to witness to others about God's love. One Saturday night sixteen hundred young people gathered at the church to sing and praise the Lord. That night many young people threw off the shackles of sin to walk in God's grace and newness of life. *That was Papa's kind of meeting!*

From the Langmo home we made contact with our Norwegian relatives. Once again we were on a train, this time to Porsgruno where my cousin Sigrid, the daughter of Papa's sister, and her husband Rolf, a stocky, earthy man with grey-blond hair and blue eyes, spoke English. His delightful humor kept us laughing most of the time.

When we arrived at their lovely home, Sigrid proved the gracious hostess, setting a picturesque table with steaming coffee and delicious apple cake. We sat around the table laughing and reminiscing as they recalled my father's visit so many years ago. Later, we met their beautiful children and their brave, young grandson who suffered massive burns in a tragic accident. His determination to live helped make medical history.

Rolf and Sigrid arranged a reunion with other cousins where we enjoyed our first delicious elk roast dinner. When we met these cousins and their families — one of them by going up a winding mountain road — we could see family resemblances. I marveled at the grace of God that kept these Norwegian people in His loving care. They, too, had come through many dangers, toils and snares. Memories of the Nazi occupation remain deep in their hearts — the years they were forced out of their homes and watched the enemy build bunkers in their lovely gardens. Their food was taken. Their men were captured and many were shot on the spot. Still they resisted!! Here and there in Norway there is still evidence of the German bunkers — rusty, iron barricades and wired fences left behind by the retreating Germans. They have these memories, but they also have memories of their bravery as they resisted the enemy.

Above all, I found my relatives to be a proud, stoic people — beautiful women, strong men, with lovely homes and gracious hospitality. Their homes shone with a scrubbed cleanliness. No wonder Mama had starched curtains even in the outhouse, and always seemed to have a beautiful sense of order. In Norway, hand-made rugs, original paintings and hand crafts of various kinds graced each home. The women were constantly hand-knitting beautiful sweaters. Even young children learned to knit.

Yes, these were my people. These were my roots. I felt a special pride in the stone fences, the gardens and the brilliant foliage of fall which reminded me of New England. The people of Norway treasure beauty — beauty in art, music and the "hidden art" that Edith Schaeffer mentions: a table, special china, a meal. Every table setting was a work of art — a change of beautiful china cups; the arrangement of assorted cheeses, meat and fish; and decoration with cucumbers, tomatoes or green pepper slices. There was even originality in the delicately folded napkins — fluffed like a flower in the empty coffee cups.

The natural resources of the country were displayed in these homes — colorful tile, marble, glass and beautiful grains of wood. The art of hand-embroidered table cloths, rugs and pillows showed not only the creativity, but the dignity of labor. I had read once that "the beauty of life is godliness. The beauty of a home is order." There in Norway, as well as in my travels through America, I could "feel" a Scandinavian home and sense the beauty of cleanliness.

Creativity was all around me. But "creation" was in the hearts of those we met. While Rolf was picking raspberries one morning, a girl asked, "Isn't that a lot of work?"

"Work?" Rolf responded. "Oh, no, a blessing from God."

On Saturday it seemed that everyone was outside, walking, jogging, bicycling or strolling with baby buggies and well-trained dogs. The stores were crowded at all times; yet, we always managed to find a corner for a coffee break.

The "walking street," famous porcelain and glass factories, beautiful stores where clerks speak English and offer helpful service — each beautiful scene was tucked away in our chest of memories.

Yet it is the people we keep in our hearts — Papa's family! Throughout his lifetime, Papa instilled in me his love of books, his love of words, his love of God, his love of people, and his love of Norway. From the moment Harold and Janice and I reached the European continent, all the Scandinavian people, the museums, the monuments, the music, the countryside were merely stepping stones to Papa's place — a journey that would help me know him better.

But before we went on to Papa's place — to the place where he was born and lived as a child — we would take a side journey to Lista, Norway — Mama's birthplace and the town where Mama's family still lives.

19

Lista

IN THE EARLY MORNING SIGRID PACKED a lunch before Rolf took us on a three-hour drive to Lista in the southern part of Norway.

We stopped at places of historical interest like the Ibsen Memorial, the famous Terje Vigen Monument and grave. Through the years Mama's rendition of Henrik Ibsen's immortal poem had made the hero, Terje Vigen, real to us. We also saw the memorial to famous pirates. This was the one that would intrigue the grandchildren when we got back to North Carolina. It would be the pirate-heroes they would want to claim as relatives.

Jan found a quaint village bakery with a coffee shop upstairs. With his sense of humor, Rolf quipped, "I always knew it was there — just didn't know where they put it."

When we forgot something, Rolf chuckled, "Somebody needs a new roof." Rolf's humor was surface and light-hearted, but his thoughtfulness and giving of time were deep. They came from a man who had lived with life and death, and faced war as a pilot — but a man who still viewed life from a positive perspective.

Along the way to Lista, we found a spot overlooking one of the many fjords where we enjoyed the lunch Sigrid had prepared, not forgetting the coffee. It was a leisurely journey with all the beauty of Norway's mountains, fjords, waterfalls, valleys and the great North Sea to enjoy.

We arrived in the city of Farsund built so long ago by the Lunds. Husan, the famous Lund residence of a bygone era, overlooked the harbor. It, too, was once occupied by the Nazi forces. Later, it became the City Hall where banquets and receptions are still held.

After touring Farsund, we drove to nearby Lista where many Farsund residents have summer homes. Lista's famous lighthouse looks out over the harbor where the North Sea stretches to England. Strong winds and mist from the sea kept us bundled in coats and scarves while we watched the waves roll over the shore of Lista. This is where my mother played as a child. The open fields, homes and barns formed a picturesque, peaceful valley. Only a few ugly Nazi bunkers left their grim reminder of war.

The North Sea, ever changing, had rolled on through war and peace. The people — these sturdy, strong-willed Norwegians — had lived through their joys and tears, planted their gardens again and re-beautified their homes. Once again lace curtains and window boxes looked out over the flowers, and the light-house kept watch over the sea as mist and wind continued to blow over the shoreline.

At 4 P.M., we arrived at the summer home of Dr. Sverre Reinertsen. We had never met before this time.

A friend from Brooklyn, New York, had sent *First We Have Coffee* to Dr. Reinertsen, a surgeon in Stavanger, Norway. When the doctor read the book, he realized we were related, and sent a letter in perfect English to me.

When he heard about our pending trip to Europe, he graciously made plans for a family reunion at his home.

The newly found relatives welcomed us to the family. Within a short time, others arrived and the house was filled with joyous greetings. As our gracious hostess, Nellie Reinertsen, served her homemade coffee cakes and whipped cream cakes, we shared our stories and memories. Jan was asked to give a rendition of Mama's favorite poem, "The Touch of the Master's Hand." Jan summed it up with a personal testimony about God's love for us. "When God tunes our lives," she said, "we make beautiful music."

Looking over these people who were a part of me, I knew God was tuning up an orchestra.

On Sunday, a grey, misty day, we joined other relatives, the Nordhassels, as well as the Reinertsens at the Vanse Kirk. It was raining when we went to church, but a quiet hush fell over us as we entered the 950-year-old historic Lutheran Church.

Generations had worshiped here. Their children had been baptized and confirmed here. And this was where Mama attended church until she was fifteen and left for America. For a few moments I pictured Mama as the four-year-old child, Elvina, and her five-year-old brother Joe sitting side by side with a relative in this old church. They were too young to understand why their mother had left for America. They only remembered her sobbing as she walked away. I could almost hear Joe say, "Elvina, we must be very good, and someday we'll go to our mother." When Joe was fifteen he left for America. One year later, Mama followed.

Now Janice, Harold and I sat beside the Reinertsens and the Nordhassels as the organ music broke the silence. Candles flickered. A young Lutheran priest in ornate robes stood in the high pulpit and opened the Bible.

I listened carefully and was able to understand my childhood language. What I didn't understand with my mind, I understood with my heart. This young Lutheran priest was speaking in the power of the Holy Spirit. His message was clear — the greatest need in the world was not food alone, but the Bread of Life, Jesus Christ as Saviour and Lord. We were one in spirit, with a desire to see a spiritual awakening, not only in Norway, but throughout the world.

After his message, we quietly followed our family to the altar where we knelt together for communion. Kneeling there, I thought of Mama. Mama had given me a good beginning. Like she had always said, "There was room at the cross for all generations past and all generations to come."

We stood for the benediction, then silently left the church.

Even in the misty rain, there was peace as we walked through the old graveyard and saw the names of generations past. I remembered again, "LORD, thou hast been our dwelling place in all generations" (Psalm 90:1).

Seated around the Sunday dinner table, we once again enjoyed the gracious Nordhassel hospitality, their lovely daughters Liv and Asta, and the red-gold-haired grand-daughter, the family's "Golden Girl."

All that day family history and stories were interwoven with the present, a blending of joy and sorrow.

Jan said, "We wanted to forget the past with its grief, but God wanted us to redeem it."

Out of the "all things" — God had worked!

We remembered the past and its sorrows with love and understanding. God had blessed many through Bertilda and Jergen Johannasen's children: Mama and Uncle Joe. In meeting Mama's family in Lista, even some she never knew, I could see the same creative love and kindness in them that was so much a part of Mama and Uncle Joe. I was proud of my heritage.

And I was proud to meet the family of the grandfather

I never knew. When I walk the sandy shore of North Carolina, I will think of him as he sailed the seas. I will recall his last lonely years walking the shores of Lista, Norway.

God has His own way of bringing blessing out of life's "all things." One day we will all meet in Heaven and sing the story, "Saved by grace . . ."

Once again — there in the land of no tears — Mama, Papa and I will sing, "Great is Thy faithfulness, Lord, unto me!"

20

Papa's Homeplace

FROM PORSGRUNO, ROLF DROVE over winding roads, through valleys and hills until we saw a sign marked *Bamble*. Then, turning around the rocky bends, we saw where the road led to a mailbox: *Tveten*. My heart skipped a beat.

Following the lane from the mailbox we saw the white, sturdy house on the right, the barns on the left. "So this is Papa's homeplace!" I exclaimed as we walked to the house where Elius N. Tveten, one of nine children, was born on May 18, 1888.

No curtains hung in the windows. No flower boxes looked out on the overgrown gardens. The sounds of living had echoed into the past.

Harold and Rolf walked around the barns while Jan and I followed a rocky trail to Papa's potato field. Nestled in the hills was a valley of rich soil where Papa had planted his gardens. Long ago, during one of Papa's rare sentimental moods, he had told me about walking hand in hand with his mother to the potato field. In the middle of planting, she had stopped and said, "Look up, Elius, and listen to the song of the potato bird." Hand in hand again, mother and son stood to listen.

I knew how Papa felt. My grandchildren enjoy working with me in the garden. In the middle of work someone will say, "Look at that butterfly," or, "Watch the squirrels," and we stop to look. Then it's back to work and the children drop cut potatoes into the holes. Kathryn decides it is faster to dump a bucketful into a hole and our dog Yenta, a yellow Lab, retrieves the hidden potatoes. We face a challenge — but the result will be potatoes for the whole neighborhood.

I could visualize my grandmother, Papa's mother, doing what I enjoy doing — walking to the garden with a child's hand in one hand, a hoe in the other.

As I stood at Papa's place looking over the valley, I saw a rocky hill like a huge boulder. That had to be the place my father had wistfully described. To him it probably had a greater significance than we could know. But the fact that he mentioned a specific place gave it special meaning to me.

Standing there, Janice and I shared our thoughts about the places we had seen: the one-room, framed schoolhouse that remained unchanged; the Lutheran church with the steeple, where the Twetens were baptized, confirmed, married and buried; the graveyard with its *Tveten* gravemarkers and memorials to past generations. We talked about the four farms where my father worked while attending school, and the four-mile, rocky, dusty road to the schoolhouse.

In my mind I heard, *You can't go home again*. But in my heart I knew *you can go home again*. I did! I came "home" to the roots where part of me belongs. I came "home" to learn a deeper understanding of how to bring the past into the present. In knowing the past, I can prepare better for the future.

The wind blew through the trees surrounding Papa's lonely childhood home. The barn was silent. The cows, chickens and horses were gone. The overgrown gardens were a reminder of another time when fruit trees blossomed in the spring, flowers grew in window boxes and the house rang with the sounds of living.

Now the wind sighed over the lonely valley as the sun lingered over the "rock" near the potato field. Reluctantly, we turned to leave. I took one final glance back over a time that is no more.

I settled back in Rolf's car and tried to imagine what life had been. Stories from the past come slowly for the Norwegian people. They carry their sorrows inside and move into the living present with patience and courage.

I was hearing stories that my father never told. Therefore, I knew the "rock" that he had mentioned had to be special to him.

Putting the bits and pieces together in my heart, I found my thoughts going back to a long-ago time, a time that could have been. I saw a young, golden-haired, blue-eyed boy running across the open field, thin coat open, hair blowing in the wind, to climb up on his "rock." With arms outstretched he shouted to the world, "I'm king of the mountain!"

This was Papa's place as a young child.

I visualized him walking slowly beside his mother later as they followed a small coffin to the graveyard. One of his sisters, his playmate, had died with the Black Sickness, a type of influenza. Papa watched the family nail a black cross on the door. Not understanding any of it, the young boy, Elius, ran to his place, to the rock. There he sobbed alone.

When spring came, the gentle mother took Elius by the hand. "Come, we plant potatoes." Living goes on.

Another day came when another black cross was nailed on the door, then another, and another, until the young Elius had seen four crosses, one after the other, nailed to the door of his home. The wind howled over the churchyard. Elius ran to his rock again and again and cried alone. Perhaps he wondered if he would be next to go in a box.

When spring came, as it always does, even after the winter of the soul, there was the cry of a newborn baby. Then a year later, there was another sound of new life.

Knute, the eldest son, helped his father till the soil and cut the timber. For Elius there was not time for play since his fragile mother needed his help to plant the garden, do the chores and care for the little ones.

Then there came another time when from the top of his "rock" he heard the sound of death — hammers nailing another black cross on the door. This time, the strong father had died. The mother, a new life within her, held the young girls while eight-year-old Elius and Knute, fourteen, watched in utter despair.

Knute tilled the land, cut the timber, and Elius tended to chores and gardens and watched over his frail mother. Once again the black day of sorrow came when the five surviving children stood around the grave of their mother. Knute was fifteen, Elius, nine, and the youngest of three little sisters was six months old.

Elius and the three sisters were taken into separate homes where they remained for several years. Elius was boarded out to four different farm homes where he had chores to complete before and after school. When he was fifteen he returned to live with Knute until he went to America two years later.

Knute, too old for his years, stayed on the farm to till the land and cut timber. He stayed until he died at the age of ninety. He had gone to the woods with his lunch pail and axe. They found him there — sitting on a log — at rest from his labors.

Years later, Papa told me how terrified he was of the dark woods around his temporary home after his mother's death. He had to carry two pails of water from the spring through the woods and couldn't run. The sounds were magnified by fear of imaginary animals and the unbearable loneliness of being separated from his family.

Papa seldom spoke of his childhood; but when he returned from his trip to Norway to visit his homeplace after forty years, he told me about the "rock" and the song of the potato bird.

"I was so lonely in those strange homes, but when I could get away, I ran for miles to go up on the rock. Then I would call out over the valley, 'Mor, Mor (Mother, Mother),' but the echo returned." I can still hear Papa saying, "I longed for the time when we planted potatoes and listened to the song of the bird. I went back to that spot when I visited Norway, and looked out over the valley. Margaret, for a moment the old grief returned," he admitted. "But suddenly, from out of the sky came the song of a bird. It seemed that the bird sang just for me. Then suddenly, it disappeared into the blue sky."

Is this when his anger built? I wondered, *back then in his lonely childhood?*

I wanted Papa to tell me more about his childhood but he shrugged his shoulders. "Ja, ja, life is a mystery," he mused. Then quietly he returned to his books.

I leaned back against the seat of Rolf's car. For days now I had traced the roots of my beginnings. But had I not also traced the roots of Papa's anger? A boy orphaned early and tossed to and fro in foster homes, a boy too old for his years? Had the anger built in his soul as each family member died, as each black cross had been nailed to the door of his childhood? I thought of Papa and his fear of the dark woods after the death of his young mother. No wonder he had learned to escape into books. No wonder he didn't go on to the university to study more, to teach. His early years had been years of responsibility.

He wasn't accustomed to following his dreams, only his chores.

But even in his childhood Papa had a rock to run to — it had set a pattern for his life. No wonder it was so easy for Papa to run to the Rock of Ages.

Before we realized it, Rolf was turning into the driveway of cousin Ella's lovely home. Inside, rustic walls held the trophies of her husband's hunting trips and the aroma of coffee already filled the room.

Beautiful handiwork and her gourmet cooking showed Ella's creativity. Around the table we enjoyed the delicious food and the love and warmth of family and friends. We shared our faith in God, and when I sang an old Norwegian song, Ella reached for her guitar. We sat together singing, Ella strumming the guitar (Himmel og jorg kan brenner). It was a song about everything disappearing — the heavens and the earth, cliffs and valleys — but the one who believes God will know that His promises never change.

When the song ended, Ella gently handed me the guitar. "This was your father's guitar," she said softly. "When he went to America, he gave it to my mother. Before she died, she gave it to me. Now, Margaret, I give it to you."

Her beautiful expression stays before me even now. I can still see her clearly as she took my hands and said in Norwegian, "You pray for me and I will pray for you."

You can go "home" again. Back to your roots, your heritage, your beginnings.

I did!

Gently, I close the lid on the treasure chest of the past. We have traveled far together — from the tent on the Canadian prairies back to the homeplace.

Now it is time to move together toward the tomorrows that are in God's hands — just as the yesterdays, with their winds and storms, sunshine and peace, were in God's faithful hands.

From the past we learn that God is faithful and the faith of yesterday rekindles faith for today. We can trust Him with the depths of our sorrows for He is acquainted with grief.

We also learn that God even trusts us, with all our frailties, to be the bearers of His love.

God's covenant and our obedience will move into the tomorrows — from generation to generation. My heart is full of praise.

Somehow, throughout the courts of heaven I hear the sound of "Amazing Grace." PAPA IS IN HIS PLACE!!!

Papa, do you see this other young man? Across the miles from glory, can you see him so like you, Papa? Blond hair blown by the wind. Clear blue eyes. Strong and sturdy — a true Norwegian. Do you see him, Papa, as he looks out over his congregation? Do you see him step behind the sacred desk?

From the open Bible, do you hear the sound of "Amazing Grace" — "For God so loved the world"?

Do you see him now, Papa — this young preacher behind the pulpit — one so like yourself? The Reverend Mr. Robert Keiter. He's your grandson, Papa. He followed in your steps.

HE TOO IS IN HIS PLACE!

Epilogue: Personal Notes

C. H. SPURGEON ONCE SAID, "Faith must make use of experiences and read them over to God, out of the register of sanctified memory, as a recorder to Him who cannot forget."

In my travels, many listeners have asked me about my living sisters.

Papa's Place has been a difficult book to write since I can share from only my perspective. Each one of my sisters could write their own story. But the more I went into the past, the more convinced I became that each one has to make a decision of the will — alone. Regardless of the storms of life, each one comes through the storm when the heart is set to live for God. We are not destroyed by the storm, but we are destroyed by unforgiveness.

Just as Papa ran to his rock in childhood, until he ran to the Rock of Ages, so each of us has to learn to stand on the sure foundation — the Solid Rock. Then the storms can come, but we still stand.

My sister, Grace, who lives in Greensboro, North Carolina, the one "God exchanged for Bernice," came through the storms still standing on the Rock. Her talents and abilities have taken her to many places, but her heart is always "home" with her sisters and their families. She keeps us all close through letters and calls.

Doris, the independent one, who always wanted to run away with Uncle Barney, came through her storms with her heart set and her feet and hands moving in obedience to the Lord. Doris and her husband Dave Hammer live up on the hill keeping watch over the valley of Stoneville, North Carolina. Their beacon light shows the way as their children, Doreen, Don, Davidson and Duane, wend their way through their own storms toward home. There they come, with their families, to the rock on the hill.

Joyce Solveig, Papa's songbird, lives in Russelville, Arkansas, with her husband Howard Jensen (Harold's brother). Together, they open their home to strangers and lonely ones. She keeps that "Scandinavian feel" in her creative touch and many couples have come to the Rock of Ages through this home.

With Howard, she has that "safe and loved" place. Their children, Judy, Paul and Steve, come with their families to rejoice in the Living Word.

Alice, Gordon's love, has come through her storms of loneliness without her husband (our brother) and reaches out with compassion and understanding to the wounded people around her.

Gordon and Alice's children, Ray, Nancy, Don and Kurt, come with their families to the place of safety, the Rock of Ages.

The youngest Tweten, Jeanelle, the one we called "Baby" in our growing-up days, lives in Ft. Lauderdale, Florida. There probably has never been a child more loved, not only by her parents, but also by her sisters and brother. To Papa, she was his shining star, the one he could laugh and talk with. Together they went to Carnegie Hall for music lessons and recitals.

Papa stood in awe of Grace and her talents but he stood amazed at his beautiful Jeanelle. During much illness as a baby, Papa carried Jeanelle on his shoulder and preached his sermons. Yet, Jeanelle remained unspoiled and loved — a special gift from God to our family. When the rest of us were gone from the home, it was Jeanelle who was still there.

Knowing how loved she was, I'm sure Jeanelle suffered more deeply when she saw Papa, the one she loved, lash out at the rest of us with undeserved anger. (Uncle Barney had always said, "There was a part of Papa no one could reach.")

The one who was loved the most has somehow suffered the most through her own storms. For her alone, Papa spent an entire night in prayer when he watched her heart breaking. She came through as gold, the gold we all hold in our treasure chest of memory. Ah, but it is not the story of storms we tell, it is the song of the soul set free. Jeanelle, through many dangers, toils and snares has come through standing on the Rock.

It was Jeanelle who spent the final moments with Papa when he was in the hospital for tests. It was at that time that the Great Communicator revealed to Papa what love he had missed — though he hadn't missed God's love.

It was Papa who always said, "Jeanelle, you are beautiful."

She smilingly answered, "That's because I take after my father."

In that final visit when Jeanelle turned to leave the hospital room, once again Papa said, "Ja, ja, Jeanelle, you are beautiful." She turned from the door to look at him. "That's because I take after my father" she repeated for one final time.

Then when Papa was alone in the room, away from the family he loved, God took him Home!

Later God spoke to Jeanelle's heart, "All My children are beautiful. They take after their Father."

Jeanelle's daughter Charlene is beautiful, like her mother. Across the miles in Texas it is Jeanelle's son Robert who stands behind the pulpit, in his place. The children come with their families to the Rock.

Since I am the eldest Tweten and have walked in God's love for many years, I have seen Mama's children reach out to bless the world — each in a special God-given way. I have also observed others who grew up in homes with ideal settings, without the winds of anger, yet I often see shipwrecked lives. Why? Perhaps there was no covenant with God.

Mama and her covenant with God stood on the Rock. Papa stood on the Rock of God's truth, and when I tremble or falter, the Rock of Ages never trembles under me.

Jesus didn't tell his disciples that a storm was coming. He simply said, "We're going over to the other side." Storms come: storms of anger, injustice, rejection, abuse, sickness or financial storms. They come! Without the Rock, Christ Jesus, we falter in quicksand. Grounded on the Rock, we can stand through the storms and come through on the other side.

Mama and Papa's children did! So will you and your children's children — if "on Christ the solid Rock" you stand, for "all other ground is sinking sand."

Heavenly Father,

Thank You for Your unconditional love for all of us, Mama and Papa's children. From my heart, I thank You for my sisters, for their love for me and love for each other.

Together, we thank You, Father, for Your gift of amazing grace.

We love You, Lord. And we rejoice, Lord, that somewhere in the courts of heaven, Bernice and Gordon join Mama and Papa in the song of a soul set free. We know — because our hearts are singing with them.

TO GOD BE THE GLORY!

The categorizing enabled us to make comparisons and generalizations later: but much more valuable were the actual replies.

Some said that citizen participation should begin with citizen knowledge about some of the more outrageous things that happen within the legislature:

> The legislative sessions are always open to the public, but except for a few hot issues, not too many members of the public ever attend. I think if they did, they would notice that there are two legislators that are always drunk and have to be led in for a vote and strapped into their seats in the direction they're supposed to vote in and immediately led out again so they won't fall off their chairs and embarrass someone. I think people ought to know this kind of thing. And I think people ought to know that this is the kind of thing that happens at 2 or 3 o'clock in the morning; some legislators hide behind their chairs so that the Speaker can't see them, so that the session has to be adjourned for lack of a quorum and really act like the worst babies you can imagine, literally playing hide and seek.

The extent to which legislators advocated more citizen participation seemed to correspond to the degree to which citizens in their district exerted pressure upon them. Many of the eighteen legislators who refused to cooperate in our Project, for example, were either unopposed completely or overwhelmingly safe in their upcoming elections. On the other hand, a former member of the House (who is now a Senator) from West Hartford represents an affluent area with numerous citizen groups and controversial issues. At the time, he was involved in a ferocious and very close campaign for the Senate. He told our interviewers that he unequivocally opposed any secret committee meetings:

A committee is a public domain. The public owns the committee. If a committee voted to kill the bill, then "to kill the bill" ought to be part of the record of the Legislature.

A co-chairman of the Education Committee, who represents an economically and racially diverse district in Hartford, has a record of openness and innovation. All of his committee's proceedings had been opened to the public, the first committee to take such a step:

Open executive meetings are going to make people get much better prepared, because they aren't going to make asses out of themselves before the press and their constituents.

Neither of these men, however, suggested that the closed-door party caucus should be eliminated. The caucus was defended down the line by almost every legislator interviewed.

That there could be no greater amount of citizen participation in the legislative process was the view of a large number of those interviewed. Again, the "safeness" of their seats seemed to play a role in how they responded. For example, an attorney who represents a largely Catholic, conservative and overwhelmingly Democratic district, many of whose constituents are employed by United Aircraft Corporation, said, "We're public hearinged to death." While stating that "I rely on local contact with constituents," he told us that "fortunately in my area, they [the citizens] do not become involved in every issue, but definitely in the issues of importance. . . ."

Citizen apathy as a rationale for taking no steps to increase involvement of the public was mentioned quite frequently. The House Minority Leader said:

Everybody ought to participate in their government...I just don't know how you can say that citizen participation can be improved by this or that specific thing . . . the average individual does not really concern himself.

He represents the very Republican towns of Bethel and Brookfield where he has not been subjected to any great amount of pressure from constituents on day-to-day issues.

A six-term veteran from the Hartford suburb of Bloomfield contended that, "there is no citizen participation" because we live in what is an "unappreciative society." And another from West Hartford said that the only citizen participation that he had seen had come from the Catholic Church and from the citizens against Interstate 291, a proposed beltway for Hartford.

Legislators as Question Marks

THE QUIET lakeside setting presented a contrast to what our first two months had been like. This Saturday morning in late July was really the first time that any of us working on the General Assembly Project had been together in other than a frantic atmosphere. About a dozen of us began this beautiful day sitting on a grassy knoll overlooking Upper Bolton Lake, about twenty miles northeast of Hartford.

The first two parts of the Project were completed. Our frenzied pace had produced an in-depth record for each legislator seeking re-election. The file included both public records and views of constituents and community leaders. Much of the boredom encountered in the first, purely research portion of the Project had worn off. But even the community work had not been terribly rewarding for some, because so few citizens knew much about their legislators. That, of course, was why we were here.

In four days we would begin a month of in-depth interviewing of legislators. Unlike the earlier stages of the Project, we could now visualize the outlines of a finished product and we knew that upon completion of the scheduled interviews, we would spend several weeks writing up the actual profiles. After that, we would have to worry about how to have the profiles produced, publicized and distributed. This lovely day, then, was really only the calm before the final series of storms.

But it was not a holiday. We were at the lake to try to insure that our interviewing of the legislators was successful. There was no doubt that this would be the most important part of the Project, for without the interviews, this would be just one more study without much value. And without key questions that probed for the most revealing responses, the full potential of our Project would not be realized.

Our enthusiasm stemmed largely from the guidance we were receiving from a Yale graduate student working on organizational behavior and experienced in both interviewing and drafting questionnaires. Richard Cech had learned about the Project through news reports and had volunteered his help.

When we had first talked to Richard, we decided to set a specific date for beginning the legislator interviews. A week after our meeting we submitted to him a list of all the questions we thought should be asked. These had been chosen from our own knowledge of legislative issues and processes and from the discussions with other groups. He took those questions, arranged them into specific categories and then inserted some of his own designed to make the respondent comfortable and willing to talk rather than to obtain specific information. At the beginning of his draft, for example, were questions like, "What has been your biggest disappointment during your service as a legislator?" and "What do you view as the most important bills you've sponsored or co-sponsored?"

In addition to helping develop questions that would elicit

the best responses, Richard also drafted an instruction sheet for our interviewers which began:

> The following outline is intended to serve as a guide during the interviews. Although you may be flexible on the exact wording of questions and although we expect you to "probe" for more specific responses in certain vital areas, you should try to adhere to the outline. It is important that you strike a balance between spending enough time on a certain issue to obtain the necessary information and getting through the interview in a reasonable amount of time.

A model introductory statement followed:

> Hello, I'm [interviewer's name]. As you heard in our phone conversation with you, I've come to talk to you about CCAG's study of the General Assembly. This interview will hopefully give you a chance to contribute ideas and viewpoints for inclusion in our final report. And it will give us the opportunity to learn more about you and verify the information we've gathered to date.
>
> (During this time you enter and become situated. Avoid chatting here and react as little as possible to efforts at humor or probing questions.)

Besides drafting the interview form, Richard convinced us to attempt to tape each interview, a very valuable suggestion. Prior to our contact with him, we had decided not to tape. Most legislators would not buy the idea, we thought, and even if they did, the presence of a tape recorder would so inhibit them that they would not give frank replies to our questions. And besides, we didn't have enough recorders, could not afford to buy any more and figured tapes would be too costly.

Our consultant changed our minds. "You're going to miss a golden opportunity," Richard said, anticipating much more than we the priceless quotes we might get. He also pointed out that our credibility would be enhanced if we could show that the profiles contained quotes transcribed directly from tapes.

Richard thought we should buy enough tapes to keep each legislator's interview on file, but we didn't have the money to buy an estimated two hundred cassette tapes, so we decided to erase and re-use some of them. The fear that some legislators would claim they were misquoted and that we would then be unable to produce the tapes bothered some of us, but it never became an issue.

Convincing the legislators that taping was mutually beneficial turned out not to be a difficult task, perhaps because of the instructions that Richard prepared:

(The only obstacle to keeping the questioning friendly is the use of the tape recorder. But raise it now in the most polite way, realizing at the same time that we want very much to be able to use the recorder.)

There's one more thing to discuss before we begin. If you don't object, I'm going to use a tape recorder. We've found that it takes less time if I don't have to jot everything down, and we'll have a much more accurate account of what you've said here.

(If he or she says it's okay, say thank you and go on. But in the event there is a disagreement, you might try a few of these arguments.)

1. Everything in this interview is "on the record" anyway, so it is not a matter of a recorder adding anything.

2. With the recorder the interviewer can listen better.

3. If the legislator is not sure, suggest that you might try the recorder for a few minutes and see how it goes. (TRY NOT TO HAVE THE RECORDER IN SIGHT WHILE YOU ARE

DISCUSSING THE MATTER, SINCE THAT MAKES IT
HARDER TO REFUSE.)

We began each interview with the section on "General
Topics" which included those questions designed to put the
legislator at ease and elicit responses about his view of a
legislator's role within the institution. Then came a section
on "Legislative and Election Issues," consisting of twelve
questions on legislative procedure, six questions on lobbying
and advocacy, four on leadership, eleven on legislative reform, eight on elections, three on media coverage of the
General Assembly and five on the role of the Executive
Branch of state government.

The third and final portion of the interview was "General
Issues." These questions covered consumer, environmental,
finance, transportation, human rights and labor issues. (See
Appendix for more details.)

With the interview questions drafted and the first batch
of blank tapes on hand, we were ready to spend a full day
with our interviewers, familiarizing them with the questionnaire and preparing them to be effective questioners. Besides
our survey expert, there were ten of us seated on the grass
who would be interviewing. For the permanent staff people
like Marty, Angie and myself there would be interviews
with party leaders and some committee chairmen. Many
of the others would interview more than ten legislators each
and would have to prepare profiles on them.

Perhaps the prospect of such a workload for the remainder
of the summer made some of the workers less than ecstatic,
but more than that, they were nervous. Certainly these
people knew more about the records of the state legislators
than absolutely anyone else—including, in many instances,
the legislators themselves. They had a good impression of
how the legislators were regarded by community leaders

and others in their districts. But research was not the same as face-to-face encounter. The closest many of the workers had come to personal contact with the legislators was in phone conversations, and some of them had felt intimidated by them. Women, especially, had been subjected to a lot of "dearie" and "sweetie" responses but, somehow, had found it easier to convince legislators that interviews should be granted. Several legislators, still upset about the letter and preliminary questionnaire sent out in late May, had either refused interviews or had said they would have to think about it. Many of the staff workers had to literally chase legislators down before they would finally say yes or no to an interview.

Quite early the legislators had realized that they were not being confronted by just another project. If they would not agree to an interview initially, we were determined to pursue them as long as there was the slightest chance that they might change their minds. Once it was clear that they were refusing, we sent them letters saying that we were sorry they had not taken this important opportunity to have their comments included in their profiles (which, we said, would be prepared and distributed with or without their assistance).

A few legislators had tried to give our workers a hard time by grilling them. "How much does Ralph Nader make?" they would ask. If the worker did not know, the legislator would often say there would be no interview until that information was made available. Others said they wanted to know our exact definition of "conflict of interests" before they would agree to an interview. We had stated that earlier and sent out more copies whenever asked.

A Hartford Representative put off Alexandra Woods for weeks. His earlier refusal to grant an interview weakened when he found that most of his colleagues were cooperating.

Even then he was reluctant. "I just know you're going to screw me," he said as he finally set a date.

Most of the workers had indeed suffered because of our firm statement of purpose in the initial letters to legislators. When added to the inferiority complex most citizens acquire when dealing with public officials, many of our workers became uneasy about the interviews. This was especially true where interviewers were going to have to ask embarrassing questions such as why some legislators tried to abolish key provisions of the Code of Ethics bill, for example, or why they said they were for coding and dating of milk products and then voted against that measure.

The need for good interviewers was obvious. Even though we were paying people next to nothing, or even nothing in some cases, we had to be selective about who was going to represent us. Those whom we felt might be too timid or who would not probe to obtain enough information were given other tasks, usually researching any additional questions that came up before or after a meeting with a legislator.

For the most part those who interviewed legislators were the same people who had contacted them initially. We felt it was important and only fair to the legislators to have them deal with one person during the Project.

We felt confident about the people we finally chose. They were outgoing, good on their feet; they could be tough, but were also personable and polite. They were not apt to be rattled by an eccentric, surly, moody or angry legislator, or by one who tried to make a joke of everything.

Richard began this late-July lakeside day by asking everybody seated around the circle what kinds of experiences they had had that might help. John Wancheck said he had been an employee of the Welfare Department and had interviewed hundreds of recipients. He also was a political science major at the University of Connecticut and had taken courses on political surveying. Miriam Frum was a former social worker for the state: Alexandra Woods, Emily Thomson and Debbie Gottheil all pointed to experiences in campaigns. And Debbie, of course, had worked on several CCAG projects while a student at Smith. Paul Shapiro's experience was also political. Angie and Marty of the permanent staff had experience as VISTA volunteers and lawyers, and my own included being a government employee and a Senate aide.

Richard's questions showed, however, that all of us had a great deal to learn. Most of it, for better or worse, would be on-the-job training; there were limitations on what could be accomplished or digested on one beautiful summer day. But the training session was extremely beneficial nonetheless, largely because it provided greater confidence for the interviewers.

Following the discussion about past experiences, we all read slowly through the drafted questionnaire (which measured more than forty pages). We eliminated some questions which were either ambiguous or unnecessary such as, "What, if anything, do you feel you have gained through your tenure in the Legislature?" and "What do you feel are your own characteristics as a legislator?" We inserted several questions from the Nader Congress Project questionnaire, adapting them to the General Assembly:

1. Applicants for federal civil service positions are required to divulge details of previous employment, salary, description of work and supervisors. Should prospective and present members of state legislatures be required to do the same publicly?

2. What do you feel is the most effective lobby in the General Assembly? How does it achieve its effectiveness?

3. Do you feel that the present make-up of the General Assembly adequately reflects the different social, racial and economic segments of the state?

From our own experience gathered during the latest legislative session, we inserted questions on both procedure and specific issues. There had been instances, for example, where bills had found their way to the House or Senate floor to be voted on without the appropriate committee members ever having heard of them. We asked this question:

Are bills ever reported out of committee without full debate and fair voting? Does this seem to be a serious problem?

We had also seen several bills, consumer ones especially, die in the Senate caucus after having been reported out of committee favorably:

Do you find significant pressure on members in the caucus to vote against their wishes? Is there too much or too little pressure to vote the party position?

But we also inserted specific questions about the legislator's own position on bills:

What position did you take on Senate Bill 41, giving additional power to the Department of Consumer Protection?

In order to make some qualifications and comparisons of responses possible, Richard suggested including a scale of categories for some questions. So, for example, on the question, "In general, do you feel there is either too much or too little party leadership control in the General Assembly?" the interviewer attempted to label the answer as one of the following: "much too strong," "too strong," "somewhat too strong," "no opinion," "somewhat too weak," "too weak" or "much too weak."

The Nader Project had submitted a massive questionnaire which required written responses to each member of Congress. Given the part-time nature of the General Assembly and its lack of staff, we stayed away from asking for much written material. The preliminary questionnaire in late May had been only one page. But we did decide during this preparation day that it would be a good idea to ask each legislator to fill out a short form either before or after the oral questioning. Richard was in favor of it basically from a procedural and psychological point of view. He felt that, if given at the very end of the interview, it would provide information we had not been able to obtain earlier because by then the legislator would be so impressed by the amount of work we had done he could not help but cooperate fully. We thought it would also give us a second chance to find out more about those elusive income statistics. The information was important, but we had also learned that compromise was an essential tool. In this case, some information would be better than none and, without seeming to backtrack, we would try to avoid further alienation and antagonism.

The short, end-of-interview questionnaire began with the following statement:

> We would like to conclude our interview with a group of short-answer questions which we believe will be easier for you to answer in written form. You may notice that some of the questions have already been answered by our researchers. In those cases, please check the information carefully to insure that it is correct. Take as long as you need and feel free to ask for clarification. . . .

(Note: Not all material from the questionnaire will be employed in the profile report. Many answers may be applied to aggregate statistics. ANY INFORMATION YOU PROVIDE HERE, HOWEVER, IS SUBJECT TO PUBLICATION OR DISCLOSURE.)

There has been a great deal of controversy generated by our earlier requests for information on income, holdings and major clients. We still believe that the public has a right to know such information. But we are willing to modify our initial questionnaire in the following way: instead of exact income, we are now requesting an "income range," and rather than major clients, are asking for major corporate clients.

With the additions and corrections made on the interview form, we began the task of preparing ourselves to conduct better interviews. Over lunch we discussed techniques such as "probing," designed to bring out as much as possible about a legislator's views and positions on issues. Our consultant kept stressing the importance of taking an opening when you see it, modifying the questions, expanding upon them and, in some cases, even leaving the written guide behind for a moment if the legislator is saying, or is about to say, something of value.

Another technique we used which was tremendously helpful was role-playing. One of us was chosen to play a state Senator with nearly twenty years' experience while another played the interviewer. To gauge the performances of the role-players, one of us was given a specific role not revealed to the others—such as a legislator who is a powerful and conservative committee chairman—and the rest of the group watched him being interviewed and attempted to guess which of several roles he was trying to play.

Throughout the Project, we had worked at getting the best

possible media exposure for our work, and today was no exception. The legislator's letter thrown in his wastebasket had provided us with an issue and we had run with it to the press. Angry responses by some legislators gave us other opportunities to let people know about the Project. Occasionally we had issued press releases listing the legislators who had been cooperative to that date. But today was not something that you could issue a press release on and expect big coverage. What would your release say? "CCAG Interviewers Prepare to Take on Legislators in Interviews." No, that would not be big news. For newspapers especially, the only really worthwhile story to come out of our meeting would have had to be a human-interest story on "How I Spent my Summer Vacation," with photographs and quotes from CCAG workers, to be used as a feature for the Sunday magazine section. And such newspaper reporting on the local level is not too common.

Television is a much better medium for our purposes, particularly with this kind of story. On a lazy summer Saturday when news has to be manufactured, this is the kind of story a local TV station loves. Channel 8 in New Haven seized upon our invitation and sent an all-too-willing film crew to the lake.

In hundreds of thousands of Connecticut living rooms that evening viewers were treated to a film of our workers sitting high on a hill overlooking a lake and engaging in role-playing. The impact on the public was probably not quite as dramatic as television coverage of the Weathermen practicing self-defense in Chicago's Lincoln Park before the 1968 Democratic Convention, but it let people know that all that talk earlier in the summer about an investigation of the General Assembly was amounting to something after all. And for legislators watching, there was a message as well: we were taking the Project very seriously and they, most of them increasingly concerned about re-election, would be wise to do the same.

All legislators seeking re-election had been contacted before the first of July for interview appointments. But even as the month came to a close, our workers were still in the process of trying to pin some of them down on a date—while at the same time preparing for the upcoming bundle of interviews already scheduled.

For those legislators who had been especially bothered by the questions on finances and conflicts in the preliminary questionnaire, we wrote and attempted to convince them to accept an interview. After giving one Representative from Bridgeport, for example, a one-page explanation of what we considered to be a conflict of interests, I wrote:

> We would greatly appreciate your opinions on this issue and others during an interview to be scheduled sometime between the 25th of July and the 25th of August. In anticipation that we may set a date for an interview, a member of the CCAG staff will contact you later this week.

With him, as with a few others, our bending-over-backward approach didn't work. He ultimately refused an interview, claiming that he did not like our definition of conflicts. "Nor can I cooperate with a group which has tried to embarrass Howard Hausman." (Hausman, a former State Republican Party chief had been appointed Chairman of the Public Utilities Commission which had recently approved rate increases for the electric companies. We had charged that Hausman, an old friend and Republican colleague of the President of Connecticut Light and Power Company, had bought the utility arguments without studying them.)

Nor was he the only Bridgeport area legislator who had refused to cooperate with us. By late July there were less than thirty out of more than 170 legislators still running for office who had said they would not grant interviews, and roughly one quarter of them were from Bridgeport.

Appearing on a local radio station's morning talk show in late July (WNAB's "Sounding Board"), I did not hesitate to present to the listeners the responses we had received from their legislators. I quoted from their letters to us or their statements over the phone. Besides the above mentioned case, one Representative had finally told our caller, "There's nothing in it for me," and another, a first-term member and attorney, had simply said, "I'm not interested."

The co-hosts of the show seemed amused but a bit uneasy with my statements. They kept asking questions like, "Are you saying that they absolutely refused to cooperate?" and "Do you think your group might have approached them in the wrong way and that is why they are not cooperating?"

I explained with what had become our standard response to that type of question. "We asked them for financial information about their backgrounds. They certainly have a right to refuse to provide that information. We, likewise, have a right as citizens to draw conclusions about their records, with or without their cooperation. And the public has a right to accept or reject our conclusions."

The hosts—and station management—were somewhat relieved when I covered them by inviting the legislators I had mentioned to call the station (this is a call-in show) and debate the issues. "If any of these legislators are listening, I wish they would call in and tell their constituents why they have refused to cooperate in this citizen study. Or if they are not listening, but someone out there knows where they can be reached, please call them and suggest that they call the station."

We received no calls from the legislators (even though I learned later that some constituents had indeed called them and suggested that they phone WNAB). At least there were no calls in the remaining forty-five minutes on the air.

Not long after, however, the three legislators just mentioned marched into the studio and demanded to hear the tape of the show. The station said that they would be happy to furnish the tape but problems arose when it was discovered that the news department had erased and re-used it.

Phil Cutting, one of the co-hosts, called me the next day in a panic. He explained that they were threatening to make legal trouble for the station. "Why don't we make another tape?" I suggested. "I'll say the same things I said on the air the first time." We then taped a statement over the phone and later that day it was played for the three men.

At my suggestion, Cutting also proposed that all of us appear on the show within a week to debate the issues. All three legislators declined. "That's just what Moffett would like," one said. "I'm not going to give him the satisfaction."

Nothing was going to change his mind about an interview. And a second man decided shortly thereafter not to seek re-election. Some Bridgeport sources told us he did not like the "harassment" he was receiving from our group. But the third Representative called John Wancheck at our office to explain that there "must have been some mistake." Wancheck had been trying to arrange an interview with him for over a month and he had refused. Now he consented.

Appearing on talk shows or generating newspaper articles turned out to be a valuable tactic in either convincing the formerly uncooperative to cooperate or, in later weeks after the profiles were completed, in getting the word out on those who had been totally uncooperative.

Late in August when it became obvious that a legislator was not going to grant an interview, he or she was sent a letter expressing our disappointment and reiterating the goals of the Project and the components of it. It then continued:

> But by far the most important source of information has been the interview with the legislator. Excluding those who have stated publicly that they will not seek re-election, all but a small minority of legislators contacted have submitted to interviews. The interviews have been helpful to both the researcher and the legislator, the former having the chance to ask pertinent questions based on the research of the previous two months and the latter having the opportunity to elaborate upon public statements or explain views on certain pieces of legislation or on the legislative process itself.
>
> It is unfortunate that you found it impossible to cooperate. Surely the legislator is in the best position to explain his or her own record, to present opinions about the mechanics of the legislative process relating to tools such as the caucus, executive session and the Code of Ethics bill.
>
> We do intend to distribute profiles on each legislator in each district before the next campaign. Although we will not have the benefit of your remarks and the clarification of your views, we will attempt to make your profile as fair and as complete as possible with the data available.

We had been telling legislators all along that the interviews would take about two hours but we really had no idea how long it would take to go through the forty-two-page interview questionnaire. The interview length would vary greatly depending, of course, on how much each legislator wanted to expound on and to what extent he showed an interest in a given area. Sections on consumer protection or transportation, for example, began with general questions like, "Do you have an active interest in the area of ... "and led to much more specific questions like, "Do you favor see-through packaging of meats?" At the end of each section were "optional" questions to be asked if time permitted and if the legislator seemed especially interested or knowledgeable in that area.

Debbie Gottheil left for her first interview and the first for the Project at about ten o'clock in the morning. She had about an hour's drive to reach Ridgefield, the home of Representative Herbert Camp. The interview was scheduled for eleven. When she was not back to the office by four, we began getting nervous. She finally arrived just after five o'clock: the interview had taken more than four hours.

The Camp interview turned out to be a little longer than average. Most took about two and a half hours, though some went as long as six. But that initial interview did a lot to boost our confidence. Listening to the tape that Debbie played back, it was obvious that we were about to compile some very valuable and intriguing information if other interviews were at all like this one.

It was also obvious even before the interview that Mr. Camp loved to talk. The computer printout on his floor statements during the past two years showed that he had spoken more than any other rank and file legislator. The floor statements reflected Camp's tendency to pick at the most minor issues, but also his wit and flowery language. The interview was no different. We were delighted to hear such statements coming through on tape:

It [publishing attendance records in committees of every legislator] would give a false sense of participation. Just being a warm body doesn't mean you're fulfilling the legislative process. . . .

On whether Connecticut students should pay tuition at the University:

I can understand no reason in God's green earth why the State of Connecticut and the people of the State should be obligated to pay the total 100% of the education of my children through college.

For most of the next month these interviews went on, from one end of the state to the other, during the day and at night, and in some pretty strange places. Researcher Paul Shapiro interviewed one Representative in the legislator's mortuary: while the questions were being asked, the funeral staff worked on corpses. One legislator insisted on meeting our interviewer on a Saturday morning in the public library of his town. But when both of them arrived, the library was closed and the interview was conducted in the legislator's car while traffic sped by on a busy street.

Emily Thomson conducted one interview in the back room of a Representative's roadside summer restaurant. She sat on a crate, he on a huge mayonnaise can. The interview lasted more than two hours. For another, the scene was the legislator's hot dog stand and the interviewer was Debbie Gottheil.

Debbie had another assignment that took place in an even more unusual setting: the legislator arranged this interview for his farm. But before it began, he insisted on taking Debbie for a tour of the property. The interview with the seventy-year-old farmer ultimately took place in an old car sitting on a back lot.

Our interviewers had been advised to seek as quiet and private a place as possible and not to accept anything more than a cup of coffee if it was offered. On numerous occasions friendly legislators offered lunch, dinner, drinks. John Wancheck was invited to a barbecue: Debbie was asked home for dinner and to meet the family. Only in a couple of cases did our workers falter, and in those instances it was almost impossible to say no. The legislators simply grabbed the checks at restaurants following the interviews and paid them. One Senator's interview lasted nearly six hours, at the end of which his wife marched in with hamburgers and beer.

One of Paul Shapiro's experiences was even wilder. Upon arriving to conduct an interview, he was told that the legislator had to stop in at a party. He told Shapiro to come along. After watching the legislator toss down several drinks in the course of an hour, Shapiro finally got his interview and ended up having to drive the legislator home.

Our interviewers were constantly being asked "What's it like to be a Nader's Raider?" This was especially true where interviews were held in legislators' homes with members of the family present.

In a number of instances the friendliness disappeared as the legislators began to realize the content of the questions. Most of them were astonished at the information we had gathered on their records and on the General Assembly overall. On more than one occasion legislators asked the interviewers, "How did I vote on that bill, anyway?" or "How many times did you say I spoke on the floor last year?"

Not all of them, of course, were as friendly as those I've just described. Some were stern, others were nasty: one member of the House even told Alexandra Woods that the study was "dangerous:"

I may think abortion is a good thing, and you people may think it's a good thing, but if you publish the answers to these kinds of questions, people like me may be out of office.

This particular Representative is known as a liberal and a hard-working legislator. But his response showed how effective and necessary our study was.

A Senator was even more blunt. "You have no right doing this," he told our interviewer. "Support of incumbents would be more in the public interest. This will be misused by challengers."

"As far as I'm concerned, you have no right to be asking these questions," another said. "But since I knew you at the Capitol, I'll go ahead."

Whatever his reasoning, we were happy to hear from him.

The Law
of Average Men

IN THE DOZENS of questions we asked in the interviews, there were two areas covered which should be of basic interest to a citizen group: who and what *are* the state legislators; and who and what influences them?

Connecticut's legislature, like most other states, contains a disproportionately large percentage of lawyers (about thirty-three per cent) and of the balance, half are educators, insurance and real estate men, business and other professional executives. More than half of the members are college educated.

Our section of the interview on elections included questions on the composition of the legislature: "Do you feel that the present make-up of the General Assembly adequately reflects the different social, racial and economic segments in the state?" and "In particular, would you like to see more representation from some particular groups, such as production workers, teachers, minorities, women, ethnic groups?"

No questions provoked more lively responses than these and few felt that a "quota system" was the answer:

When you have an elected body, you have to assume that the constituents have put these people there on the basis that they are going to best reflect the views of the constituency or the district they represent. I have always been a believer in letting the voter make the ultimate decision. ... Unless you're setting up a quota system for the Legislature and throwing out the elective process, you can never be sure that somehow there wouldn't be a more representative group. ... Whether or not a Black might be more representative of a particular district than the guy's now in there, you just don't know.

Another Representative reacted strongly to the question:

If you're talking about a quota system, no. Because obviously when you've got 18 women out of 177 (members of the House), that doesn't reflect the percentage of women in the population. ... But I don't feel that because I am a woman I must represent women. I prefer to be thought of as a legislator who represents a district. Yes, I would like to see more women, but I think it's up to them to make the effort to get in. I certainly would hate to see the point where we say 50% of our legislators have to be women. 'Where can we put in another female; oh come now, we've got to get one from someplace.' And suddenly you drag up this kook who has done nothing. That is what quota systems do and I think that degrades the whole system.

Numerous legislators contended that all segments were adequately represented, though not arithmetically:

The whole assumption of this question is wrong. Even though the actual people elected may not be from a particular social, racial or economic segment, there is a near balance because they take views which assist those groups.

and:

I'm for representation by anyone who will do a good job, black, white, yellow. But generally I think there is adequate representation of the full spectrum of Connecticut citizens.

One of the leading proponents of womens' rights in the General Assembly, who is a man, said:

I used to want more women [in the legislature] before 10 out of 18 voted against the Equal Rights Amendment. That's a good example of how young people don't necessarily represent young people, Blacks don't necessarily represent Blacks, and so forth.

Another did not regard "mathematical representation" as important. He thought that the legislature was representative of a broad spectrum of the public in other ways:

We've got a lot of people who work in factories; we've got a bricklayer. But you don't have to be a bricklayer to know what a bricklayer is thinking, if you take the time to find out.

A Representative regarded as a loyal party organization man took the occasion to aim a surprising slap at State Party Chairman John Bailey:

Some of these guys are no more equipped to know what the average guy is thinking ... I think maybe I do: I go eat in my brother's bar at lunchtime. I see five or ten fellows who either work in the factory or drive a truck, or something like that. I think I know what they're thinking. But John Bailey probably hasn't talked to a truck driver in 20 years, unless he's backed into one. . . . So the guy from Westport, the legislator who knows only arty people or people with money, he and I balance each other out.

Most legislators did not pretend to be the "average guy" themselves, but did feel that they represented him. "Who represents the average man? Not the average man."

However, a few of those interviewed asserted that representation of those who were not "average" was inadequate. "We do a good job of representing the middle strata," said one. Another, a powerful party political figure, blamed the lack of representation mainly on low salaries. He said it has become harder, not easier, in the past ten years for someone to challenge him or any legislator in a district:

We have a higher poverty level, but in addition to the financial aspect, there is the political setup . . . you get endorsed by a Town Committee which is pretty much self-perpetuating . . . I have repeatedly told the minorities that they should learn that the way to power is to control the Town Committee.

The salary level appeared to be only part of the larger problem of the legislature. The question of adequate representation for all races, for women and for all income groups seemed to be tied very closely to the need for a full-time lawmaking body. A majority of those interviewed told us that they are working full-time on legislative matters now, but are not being compensated for it:

Government doesn't stop on the first Wednesday after the first Monday in June in the first year, nor does it stop after three months in the second year [the time periods that the legislature is in session]. Interim activities are important but you really don't have three co-equal branches of government when we're not in session.

But this particular legislator warned that making the General Assembly full-time would not automatically increase representation from other than the "middle strata:"

> Nationwide examples would show that if anything, it narrows the base. You have more lawyers and more professional people going into it, even in states like California, Michigan and Illinois. You have fewer neighborhood people going. Your quality, I believe, improves, the staff services improve, the resources improve, but you don't broaden the base.

Is it possible, we asked, to make the legislature full-time and still broaden its base? Yes, was one reply, but:

> You're going to have to go out and recruit people and encourage people to move into the arena to make them feel that it's not something that is the exclusive province of just the lawyer or realtor or insurance man.

In the few other states that have gone "full-time" and found that less proportionate representation was the result, it is important to note that they were paying salaries of more than twenty thousand dollars per year. Some of the legislators who told us they favored a full-time legislature said they thought salaries should be at least twenty-five thousand dollars. But a few contended that it was precisely a salary level of that kind which would make the post attractive enough for professionals to spend great sums of money to gain a seat, while the average person would be unable to compete. A more realistic salary level, they said, might be around fifteen thousand dollars per year.

Among those legislators who said they opposed a full-time legislature, the most common complaint was that it would create a group of "professional politicians" who would lose contact with the daily life and problems of their districts:

You'd end up with a whole different breed of people. .... At $12,000, you'd get people who had a lot of money, or people who might be incompetent and poor. It's not for the best. You'd end up with people looking for a home; they'd become less responsive and more arrogant. Because if you were there full-time, you wouldn't be able to gather the kinds of thinking or have the kind of back-home contact that you have to have now. I couldn't live on that kind of money. You would get either very wealthy people or those who couldn't do anything else, but might be able to get themselves elected.

And from another, conservative Representative:

Connecticut's been well-served by a citizen-legislature, unlike other places, like Texas. We've never had, that I'm aware of, an instance of corruption in state government or guys on the take. That's because we've had a citizen-legislature. We haven't got a situation where they rely on this for their living.

A state Senator said that he sees the need for a full-time body. "You'd get more ordinary citizens if you bring the salary up to the twelve to fifteen-thousand-dollar level." But, he said, there is one thing about the example of other states that bothers him:

California has a full-time legislature, and they're rated number one in efficiency and salary. My own feeling is that full-time has meant there is also full-time fund-raising and campaign expenditures. A hotly contested race for the state legislature costs between $150,000 and $200,000. That scares me.

When we asked about how the composition of the legislature should be changed, "Get rid of some of these lawyers," many of the non-lawyers said. A stonemason noted, "People have a tendency to lean towards the lawyer before they would lean toward the working man. It's ridiculous, but I think they're beginning to realize that now."

An outspoken Senator fumed when we asked him about more representation for minorities:

> I resent being told that I can't represent minorities. You've got 66 lawyers. That's a cross-section? I don't think they reflect the people . . . I'd like a better cross-section, but I'm not talking about the ethnic thing.

Perhaps it was not reasonable to expect such a male-dominated body (there are twenty women among the 213 members of both the House and Senate) to suggest that efforts should be made to encourage more women to seek election to the legislature. Very few of those interviewed actually referred to the potential of large numbers of well-educated women who might be available. An elderly Representative from a small town in the eastern part of the state summed his feelings up this way:

> There should maybe be more women . . . but women and women don't get along . . . men can agree on things.

Special interest lobbies have had a tremendous impact on the actions of state legislatures. Connecticut has been no different. Listed on the Secretary of State's roll of registered lobbyists are people representing, among others, the Connecticut Roadbuilders, Northeast Utilities, the insurance companies, Connecticut Bankers' Association, J.C. Penney's and the Soft Drink Association. According to the House Assistant Majority Leader:

> Sometimes a piece of legislation would appear mysteriously on the calendar and none of the leaders knew how it got there. So in order to smoke out who is interested in the legislation, we would put the bill at the foot of the calendar [postponing action on it] and I would be given the assignment of strolling around the hallways of the Capitol waiting for someone to approach me to ask why the bill was put at the foot of the calendar. Then we'd know who was pushing the thing.

It is common knowledge that in addition to speaking with legislators in the Capitol building hallways, lobbyists discuss legislation while entertaining them at lunch, dinner or special functions. It has been mentioned to us how frequently "hospitality suites" spring up in hotels near the Capitol as the legislative session nears an end and important legislation approaches the top of the calendar. The utility companies host the Banks and Regulated Activities Committee members (utilities legislation comes before this committee) for cocktails, dinner and "informal discussion." The Connecticut Roadbuilders throw a similar bash for the members of the Transportation Committee. Although some legislators told our interviewers that no legislation is discussed at these functions, several Representatives said that they avoided certain social functions "because they smacked of a payoff."

Among the questions we asked about lobbyists were:

1. Connecticut has legislation to regulate in some ways the activity of lobbyists. Is enforcement of this legislation adequate, in your opinion? Why or why not?
2. In what ways, if any, do you find lobbyists helpful?
3. Can you give some examples of how pressures are brought

to bear on you by lobbyists? Do you find any specific tactics objectionable?

4. Do you make any distinction between a lobby for profit-making interests and a citizen lobby?

Most legislators appeared to regard lobbyists as a fact of life at the Capitol, although the consensus seemed to be that leadership, much more than the rank and file, was under the gun from special interests:

Lobbyists are more of a problem for leadership than the guys on the floor. I haven't had many problems; not that lobbyists are not guilty as charged . . . they are not necessarily bad guys. . . . They can be a good way to get information although sometimes they try to add two and two and get five.

Another said he has never had any problem with lobbyists:

I tell them where I stand on a bill and they leave me alone: . . . Any lobby has a point of view they're pushing. They all convince themselves that certain legislation is needed for the good of the state.

And from our outspoken Senator quoted earlier:

We don't need our time taken up by lobbyists hassling you individually . . . on your back, dunning you to death . . . Bankers, making $50,000 to $60,000 a year, acting like a bunch of guttersnipes.

Several other legislators seemed resentful of the large sums of money made by many of the lobbyists:

As a legislator who is not being paid much money, I very much resent the efforts of lobbyists who are paid far more than we, who bring in information that is not always straight.

Information tainted with the bias of a special interest seemed to be the largest complaint about lobbyists. Only a few legislators referred to strong-arm tactics. "I don't like to be pulled into a corner," and from another, "I tell them to go to hell." One Senator spoke about the need to stop "the gesticulating from the doorway" leading into the House. Evidently, more than a few legislators resent lobbyists giving signals on how to vote. And in some cases, lobbyists have not been content to stay outside the chamber. House Speaker Ratchford has been praised by most legislators for his firm stand in having lobbyists ejected from the chamber after they had sneaked onto the floor.

But generally we were given the impression that pressure is almost entirely directed at party leaders to begin with, especially majority leaders:

[Only] when they find that leadership won't take a position, then they go to work on the rank and file in both Houses.

Some rank and file seemed genuinely surprised by our questions about lobbyists' pressure: they simply had never experienced it. But most who had dealt with the lobbyists felt that they provided an important source of information as long as they remembered that some of the information was biased.

"Probably the biggest experts in the world on what they're discussing," is the way one Representative described lobbyists. "I've never been double-crossed by their information," we were told by another, a veteran of three terms in the House. "You're like a judge listening to both sides," said a Senator.

From one legislator who has been in a position to be pressured:

> They [lobbyists]' try to be both entertaining and informative. If they want to take me out to lunch, I'll go out and eat their lunch, and it won't affect my vote. I've made it a practice to try and reach an early decision on legislation, then a lot of pressure groups leave me alone.

Not all legislators, of course, were as candid in telling us about lunching with lobbyists, but most said it was important to know "where the lobbyists are coming from."

"I don't want to cut off a source of information, even if it is biased," said a Representative who is also an educator. Indeed, with the lack of staff and time as well as other limitations imposed by the part-time nature of the General Assembly, most legislators feel they could not do without lobbyists. On the other hand, we were told by some that "very few lobbyists provide meaty information. Their effect on a particular issue is minimal, absolutely minimal."

In describing how he makes a decision on a certain bill, a freshman legislator said:

> I read the bill. I have an opinion on it from reading it. If not, I talk to someone from town, if there's time. If it's coming up fast, I talk to other legislators. The library doesn't help. Legislative research is okay in long-term matters. Lobbyists come about last.

One who had perhaps the best vantage point from which to view the activities of lobbyists at the Capitol was Speaker William Ratchford. He had, before our interview, made public his proposals for stricter regulations of lobbyists, including the wearing of badges in the Capitol hallways:

The lobbyist abuses during the 1971-72 session were the worst I have observed during my ten years as a legislator. The harassment of legislators both inside and outside the chambers reached an intolerable level and will be prevented by the legislation I am proposing.

Ratchford had at one point proposed keeping lobbyists off the second floor (where the House meets) altogether, but his idea was criticized by both legislators and lobbyists. The Majority Leader at the time had asserted to our interviewer that self-policing was the answer:

Keeping lobbyists off the second floor is nonsensical. The only effective way to cope with lobbyists who take advantage or want to is through self-restraint and by imposing your will on them. If it's somebody you don't want to be associated with, you avoid them.

Ratchford, by the time of our interview, was no longer pushing the second-floor ban. But he was still just as firm on the need for regulation:

I don't think that [it's] constitutional ... What we may have to do is have a rail to keep them back from the door. I had hoped that the more responsible lobbyists would say "Hey, let's try to start policing ourselves," but unfortunately I've gotten some very defensive letters which shows that they're not as sensitive to the public attitude on this. There is no way the lobbyists are going to win in a public fight, no way. And yet they feel "our pride, our integrity, you are challenging almost our honesty by making these proposals."

Of the 134 legislators interviewed, forty-three per cent

said that they thought a citizen lobby should be regulated differently from a profit-making lobby, while forty per cent said all should be treated the same.

The CCAG's position on this point has been that distinctions between lobbyists are impossible to make legislatively. In February of 1973 we filed suit in the U.S. District Court in Hartford to have the current law requiring a lobby fee declared unconstitutional as an obstacle to the exercise of a First Amendment right—much the same as the poll tax. On June 21, a three-judge federal panel upheld our claim. But we have consistently maintained that a citizen lobby does have a different point of view from one representing industry. Some legislators, however, did not agree with our viewpoint:

> To suggest that the citizen lobby presents a point of view other than that of lobbyists themselves is, I think, well . . . that takes a tremendous amount of ego . . . the CCAG is an elitist operation because it is doing for people what [people] don't care whether or not is done for them. Because if they really cared, you wouldn't be broke. . . . I disagree wholeheartedly with the philosophical concepts of the elitists of this world.

Only a little less blunt was another response:

> The problem you have with, quote, public service groups, unquote, such as yours is that if you say that public service groups are not covered by a certain regulation, then anybody can become a self-anointed public service group and lobby.

Some legislators went so far as to say that they were more troubled by citizen than by industry lobbyists. We were told by one, "I don't like being grabbed in the hall." But he wasn't pointing his finger at industry lobbyists:

Last year [1972] it got out of hand—not the professional lobbyists, but other groups, such as citizen groups, the League
of Women Voters, teenagers, unions. The regular lobbyists don't
give you too much trouble.

Although one Representative felt that "Lobbyists are
experts. You can use them as a source of information. They
know their area and they are an excellent source," he went
beyond this to suggest that citizens should not be among
those lobbyists at the Capitol:

Constituents know where you live—they should go to you there,
not approach you in the halls of the House. It's hectic when
they come here.

Leadership, party leaders and the pressure they exert upon
the rank and file was another area we needed to know more
about.

In a part-time legislature, the power of party leaders
determines virtually everything that happens. Professional
staff assistance available to them places them steps ahead
of other members in terms of information at their disposal.
Many rank and file legislators are lucky to know which
bills are coming up on a given day, let alone the relative
merits of opposing arguments on the bill.

Control of the gubernatorial office has a major influence
not only on the incumbent's party itself, but also on the
machinery of that party: when the word comes down to
the party leaders, much of the arguments and discussions
on where the party should stand have already been decided.
This is obvious in every state capitol, but more so where
the governor is a nationally known and influential politician.

Considering that our interviews were held among the

legislators of only one state and were all either Democrats or Republicans, it was amazing how many points of view were expressed, and how different were the experiences with leadership. The opinions ranged from "too influential," "too weak" or "just right," to thoughts that something was right or wrong with the governor's men, the caucus system and ˉor the party chairman. Those who felt that leadership was too strong, however, were more vocal than their opponents.

From our maverick (Republican) Senator quoted earlier:

> The absolute subservience of House Republicans to the Governor is the most disgusting. The Democrats used to be as bad. I'm a long time advocate of co-equal branches of government. I'm not on very good terms with either my party or the Governor because I don't believe in subservience. ... The Governor doesn't exactly candy to people who try to tell him what is going on and warn him of the consequences of his action. He's a yes man, he loves yes, yes, yes, yes

A political science instructor and Republican Senator wasn't quite so blunt on conforming to party pressure:

> You can only be the skunk at a garden party for just so long, even if you're very sincere about the stands you take. You get the feeling that your colleagues are beginning to view you with annoyance. You're just not one of the gang after a while.

When we asked a two-term legislator who has not been considered "one of the gang" what she thought of the party caucus and the leadership exerted therein, she said:

> The caucus is a ridiculous waste of time, and doesn't accomplish anything. The leaders come in and tell you what's going to

happen ... It's a joke. Those idiot legislators stand up and ask the same dumb questions every caucus.

Another Republican and one of the senior members of the House has spent more than fourteen years in the legislature. His sense of independence was reflected in his statement to us on the party caucus:

Caucuses aren't like they were a few years ago. Then you could get up and object without being ridiculed. Now, if you don't go along with dictation, you're this and you're that.

It was also stated like this: "There's something to be said for party allegiance [but] it's more important to have individual integrity."

There is subtle but significant pressure in that you know if you vote against the Governor, you will be treated at some distance. The only thing a legislator has going for him is the troops as opposed to the leader. The people back home vote you in.

Not all disenchantment with the performance of leadership is limited to Republicans, of course. A young Democratic freshman who was subsequently reapportioned out of his seat spoke of the actions of a fellow Democrat, House Majority Leader John Papandrea:

Most of my conflicts were with him. I call him the "confidence man," the "hatchet man," for the Democratic leadership. There was an occasion when I was on the Transportation Committee and there was a leadership bill that was really his baby. I opposed the bill in committee and it never came out of committee, and the Chairman got it in the neck from leadership because he let the bill die, and he said, "Bill Ryan did it," and Papandrea openly did a job on me.

Representative Papandrea responded to those charges:

I would resent any feeling that I have been the hatchet man, not ever having been the hatchet on my own. I've had to be the guy that has gone out and done some of the unpleasant tasks. My own history has always been fighting for what I always believe is right, and I draw the line at party discipline as long as the guys are not playing screw around. You know that's one thing, but when a guy is furthering his own matter of conscience that's completely another. I think on the outside, it's very difficult to tell where one ends and the other begins. Someone has to find out because there are two types. People who come up here masquerade as really crusading for something, but all the while they are really jockeying for something on their own and could care how disruptive it is on the ability of the party to act.

Papandrea told our interviewer that he had never had much of a reputation as a party person:

I came up through the primary route and was very much of an iconoclast of my own before it was fashionable to be that way. But I think party discipline isn't exerted more than 3 or 4 times in a session since I've been here. But you've got to have it, otherwise, what the hell is the sense of having a party.... I don't have a group of legislators that I'm responsible for. I do have a specific number of the members of the caucus assigned to me. Unfortunately, I've been relegated to the position of having to do more [arm twisting] than I would like.

A liberal Hartford Democrat representing a middle-income constituency said that, "Democratic party caucuses are . . . essentially perverted into an institution which leadership uses to beat people into line." He had made strong attempts to have the party support an income tax bill, but had been rebuffed each time.

A seven-term Democratic veteran of the House known for his outspoken views on behalf of the consumer agreed with those who claimed that leadership pressure in the caucus was too strong:

> I would call it ineffective and I would object to it. I attend very few of them. I don't think the . . . caucus is as democratic as it could be. . . . I'd rather not feel the pressure to vote. . . . Well, they don't break your arms, they don't threaten to shoot you. They give very little credence to the objectors—those who may not agree, and it is quite an embarrassment, frankly.

Another who had taken her lumps on the income tax, a former college economics instructor, was asked whether she had ever been retaliated against for disagreeing with leadership and she replied:

> Yes, indirectly. I was pressured in the first session by leadership on the income tax. I received a phone call, and was told in blunt terms that everything was over, goodbye to everything I wanted to do.

On occasion the party can prevent a person from obtaining a nomination and thus deny the folks back home even that chance. What is more common, however, is making it tough on the legislator within the legislature itself. One Republican Representative answered our question on whether party leadership ever retaliates for uncooperative rank and file:

Yes, by getting innocuous committee appointments. But it is more political than legislative. I supported Clark Hull for Governor and then supported Barnes in the primary. Meskill didn't care for this. But being a politician, I don't place any blame there.

An Assistant Democratic Majority Leader in the House at the time confirmed that retaliation is taken inside the General Assembly chambers against legislators who resist the party line:

> You pay the price in terms of [a committee] not reporting out your bill. [Then you] have to use devious means—like getting someone else to sponsor the bill.

But members who told us that there was either too little leadership or just the right amount greatly outnumbered those who asserted that leadership was overbearing and retaliatory. A dairy farmer and ten-year veteran of the General Assembly said:

> You can't have democracy without party leadership. 300 guys can't go their own way all the time.

An attorney and Democratic Representative said:

> We get free rein. ... You almost have to press him [the House Speaker] to ... let you know when there's a position that is considered part of the Democratic platform.

There were a few legislators who said that the rein was indeed *too* free, that their party leaders provided no direction, little information and less organization.

Well-known as an environmental advocate and free-thinker, one legislator who is an author of educational publications might have been expected to tell us that the leadership was too strong. But his description of how his own party leaders had performed was:

> Poorly, let me put it to you this way, very poorly. One of the greatest weaknesses that I have seen in the past two years is the lack of communication between the Democratic party leadership and the membership of the House.

One of the most outspoken legislators on leadership cited an incident in which the party leaders had tried to be strong and wound up appearing only strong-armed:

> [In 1969] there was an area that I wouldn't go along with, so the leadership removed $5 million from my Route 8 project as a punishment which I promptly denounced on the floor of the House and got my $5 million back. That kind of thing is childish. We're not up there to be the tail wagging the dog.

And finally: "You have to have this political input; an individual legislator cannot keep up with 7,000 bills himself."

What did the leaders have to say when we asked them about the various opinions the rank and file offered us on their performance? (We had interviewed most of the members before the leaders' interviews so we could ask specific questions in these latter cases and have substantive comments to back them up.)

The former Majority Leader and now Minority Leader of the House said that making himself available to members is one of his most important functions:

My role specifically is to make sure members know what is being voted on. You inform mostly through face-to-face conversation. . . .But there are no threats. And except for things like the budget, we very seldom ask for a party vote. But I might be able to manipulate the situation better than the average rank-and-file guy.

His counterpart on the Republican side, the fellow who had thrown our initial letter in the wastebasket, advised his rank and file members to do the same. Nearly two months after that incident in a most candid and cordial interview, he was asked about charges that he attempted to impose the Governor's will on his members, and that he would take retaliatory measures against recalcitrants:

I have more respect for individual legislators than to do things like that . . . it's not my nature. . . . No matter who they are and what you think of them, personally, you have to realize that one of the reasons that people sent them up here was to exercise their judgment.

Oh, we kid people a lot, guys, for example, like Joe Vella. Joe says to me sometimes, "Gee, I've got a tough district, I gotta vote with the Democrats on this one". . . . And I keep saying, "Jesus, Joe, you're really gonna have problems, you know. You gotta be with the party once in a while." . . . Jokingly it's been done, but no attempt has ever been made to sit a guy down and say, "Look, you're going way out of line and you're gonna be in trouble." I've never seen that happen in 6 years in the Legislature.

William Ratchford, Speaker of the House at the time of our study, was probably the best-known, most vocal, youngest and most politically ambitious leader in the entire legislature. He claimed that an important ingredient in his kind of leadership was making himself available to the rank and file members. In our three-hour interview with him, we raised specific charges about weak leadership. He minced no words in his reply: evidently he had thought about those charges before:

I think I know my people very well. I spend a lot of time. I'm there at seven-thirty quarter to eight in the morning. I'm one of the last people to leave the building ... and I'm talking to people all day long. I think I know their constituencies; I think I know what they can and cannot do, realistically. And I usually call on them for a vote when I feel that I need it. I'm not someone to put the arm out all the time. I'm not built that way.

Warts and All

THERE WERE PEOPLE who thought we were out of our minds when we announced that the legislators whose profiles were to be included in the Project would be invited to look them over before they were printed. Actually, the idea had come from the Congress Project, but we could see the value for and to ourselves.

The opportunity to see the first drafts would allow the legislators to point out any "factual" errors in our work. This would put the Project in a good light as far as the public was concerned and cover us in the event that any mistakes had been made. If a legislator declined our invitation and later discovered an error, we could at least say we had given him a chance to correct it, and he had turned it down.

At first we thought we would try and reserve a room at the State Capitol, but later decided to invite the legislators to our offices. Our decision was based more on the difficulty of transporting the files and other materials to the Capitol each day than on anything else. More than sixty out of the one hundred and fifty people on whom we had prepared profiles showed up. A few others had their profiles read over the telephone. The looks on the faces of many of them as they climbed the steep stairway to our second-floor, run-down suite of offices was something to behold, many asking themselves, "What the hell am I doing climbing these stairs in this crummy place?"

What they were doing there, as all of them knew, was examining what we had written about them and what it was we planned to release just before election day.

When each legislator arrived, he or she was seated at a desk with a yellow legal pad and handed the edited draft. "Please make any suggested changes on the yellow pad and not on the profile itself," we would ask them. "If you have any questions, please let us know." We also offered coffee and tea when our worn-out percolator was working.

There were looks of astonishment when the legislators were handed their profiles. It was obvious that such an in-depth piece of work had not been expected.

"Profile?" said one. "You call this a profile? This is a goddam treatise!"

The reactions of those who came to the office to view their profiles were varied. Some wanted drastic changes made. Some demanded that we not print their profiles at all. Others were amazed at how fair we had been.

A member of the Senate came in to read his profile and became extremely upset when he read the comments that he "cares only about the rich people in [his district]," as well as statements claiming that he was not a strong leader.

"This is the worst thing that's ever been written about me," he told me over the phone. I assured him that we had not invented those comments, that they had come from actual statements, but that we would also gladly place his rebuttal in the profile.

In a couple of other situations we allowed legislators to rebut statements that had been made by others in their profiles, but in many cases we didn't or couldn't—either for reasons of space, or our knowledge that the rebuttal statement was contradictory to the facts. Some had forgotten that they had already rebutted.

One Representative was nothing less than livid when he saw his draft. He was, at that time, an associate of a law firm which did a great deal of business with state agencies, representing clients before the Banking Commission, Liquor Control Commission, Real Estate Commission, among others. In 1971, the General Assembly had passed a Code of Ethics bill which prohibited members of the legislature or members of their law firms from practicing before such agencies. The reasoning was sound. Even subconsciously, commissioners of such agencies might bow to the wishes of lawyers who are also legislators or who work in firms with legislators. After all, legislators control the purse strings which dangle in front of these agencies each year.

We had alleged in his profile that this legislator had led a surreptitious move to abolish that prohibition. He had denied it. But we had corroborated it from statements submitted to us by other legislators, by members of the press, by private attorneys and others. In his visit to our office, he insisted that we not release that portion of his profile dealing with the ethics bill, nor other portions which he claimed were inaccurate, such as our contention that for a big city legislator, he had not demonstrated any great interest in the important issue of mass transportation.

Another Senate leader came in, read his draft, asked for only a few minor changes and left. Several hours later I received a call from him. "I've been thinking about it. I don't think I was tough enough on the Commissioner of Transportation," he said. "Can I put in some stronger language?" I told him that his profile had already gone to press.

We found that few of those who had allowed their interviews to be taped complained about the quotes in their profiles. Taping had definitely been an excellent idea. But there were a couple of exceptions, one who had been told prior to his interview, as were all the other legislators, that everything was on the record and that he would have an opportunity to make factual corrections of the draft before it went to press.

On a day in early October, this exception came in to read his profile. Whenever a legislator was in the office, we made it a practice to bend over backward to answer any questions or complaints. In this instance, I happened to be walking by as the legislator was complaining to one of the staff members. I stopped to see if I could be of help, only to find that he wanted some of the transcribed quotes changed.

"Are you saying that you didn't say the things that you're quoted as saying?" I asked.

"No, I said them, but the young lady who interviewed me said that the quotes would not be put down exactly as they were given, that we'd have a chance to change them."

"Well, that doesn't seem right," I replied. "Our policy has been that you can change factual errors, but not quotes. Which ones do you want to change?"

He had a number of them copied down on his yellow pad. He pointed to a sentence relating to legislative processes in which he had been quoted as saying, "They talk about up-dating, modernization, and all this other hanky-panky. I call it that because it sounds good and people love to hear it, while they aren't achieving what they should be."

"What's wrong with that?" I asked.

"What's wrong with it? It sounds terrible. I would never

have put it that way if I had known it was going to be a direct quote."

From those few who had not allowed their interviews to be taped, there were numerous charges of misquotations.One Senator had told a colleague, "I can't believe you let them tape you. How could you do that? I'd never let them get me on tape." It wasn't that he had much to hide; it was rather an uneasiness about being taped.

The section of the profile which brought the most opposition from legislators was the service to constituents section. While this was our weakest portion in terms of supporting data, it was also important to give the reader a view of how the legislators were seen by community leaders.

A Representative complained that it was unfair to quote an individual whom we identified as "an advocate of mass transit" or "a member of a civic association" who said that he was not responsive to the need for mass transit. He insisted that we either identify that individual or remove the statement from his profile. We did neither.

A few legislators, unhappy over what they viewed as potentially embarrassing and politically damaging information in their profile drafts, resorted to using third parties to attempt to have the controversial statements deleted. A Representative from Fairfield County had been accused of owning some wetlands property while at the same time working in the legislature against a proposal to protect such areas from development. In our interview with him, we asked about this and included in the drafted profile an explanation of the charges and his responses.

Since the Representative did not have time to come to Hartford to read his drafted profile, we agreed to read it over the phone to him. A short time later, Angie received a call from the president of another consumer association. He was calling to try to convince us that we should take the wetlands discussion out of the profile. Angie refused. He then called me.

"[This legislator] has really been a strong advocate on consumer bills," he told me. "It will just hurt him and he won't be so helpful to all of us next year." Like Angie, I said we would not consider the deletion, that the information was factual, most of it from the horse's mouth.

Similarly, another legislator tried to influence us to have a statement removed from his profile which was made by a League of Women Voters member accusing him of being a late-comer to a local fight against an expressway. Again, the result was the same.

Some legislators came really expecting the worst. One Representative who is now a state Senator represents a district that is mostly Republican and affluent. Almost every piece of research on him indicated that he was a solid performer for his district. Comments from community leaders, even those who disagreed with him philosophically, were favorable. His communication with constituents was mainly through a regular, lengthy and often esoteric newspaper column. When important and controversial local issues arose, he was there. And people appreciated it.

His profile, then, appeared to be very favorable. I remember watching him reading it in the midst of thousands of profiles and clanging mimeograph machines with a wide smile on his face, saying, "I can't believe how fair this is!"

The Senator whose interview had lasted somewhere around six hours came in joking as usual. Like most of the others, he appeared to have little idea of the depth of our Project. I personally handed him the draft of his profile and invited him to use the table in my office to review it. "Let me know if you have any questions," I told him, closing the door to give him some privacy. I walked into the next room where a few staff members were talking.

Suddenly from my office we heard a roar of laughter. The bellowing would stop momentarily and then start again. This went on for about half an hour. Finally I walked in, right in the middle of another outburst.

"Hey, this is great stuff," he said. "I really come out with some great lines, don't I?"

Representative Camp, who had been interviewed first, had asked Debbie Gottheil at the time for a copy of his transcribed statement when available. But we wanted to make sure that none of the remaining 150 legislators saw the questionnaire form before they were interviewed.

A couple of weeks later we received an emotional letter from him demanding a copy of the statement and referring to CCAG's "outrageous" conduct. I called him on the phone and again promised him that the other interviews would be completed shortly and we would furnish him with a copy of his statement. He exploded:

> You are a bunch of unfair, deceitful people. I know what you're up to . . . you're going to smear me.

And on August 18, he wrote to the House Minority Leader:

> I think other legislators should be warned not to make statements to this group. I very much hope that you will undertake to warn our colleagues.

All of the above was written into the introduction of his profile. When I saw him coming up the stairs, I cringed. We fetched his draft from the files, sat him down and scattered to different sections of the office. After about fifteen minutes I forced myself to stand in the corridor so I could see into the office where he was sitting. There he sat with a "Boycott Lettuce" sign above him and our two

Siamese cats curled up on the desk. He was reading the profile with obvious delight. Looking up he noticed me and said, "This is okay." He was still grinning. I later took him on a tour of the office to show him how the profiles were being put together.

"You realize that you spoke more than anybody else on the House floor in the past two years," I told him. I then related that his computer printout on floor debates stretched clear across the floor. He asked to see it. Holding up the printout, his eyes shone; the paper was lumped in a big pile on the floor. "Just think," he said. "The taxpayers get all these statements for just three thousand dollars a year."

Getting It All Together

THE REAPPORTIONMENT BATTLE that had been going on between the two major parties for months was now mired in the courts. There was talk about the November elections for the General Assembly being postponed until the U.S. Supreme Court ruled on the matter (which would probably result in either January, 1973, elections or the entire legislature being "held over" for another two-year term).

Along with a number of other groups (some of us unlikely allies) including the Connecticut Business and Industry Association, the League of Women Voters, the Council of Churches and the Women's Political Caucus, we attempted to convince a federal court that elections should be held, based on state and federal constitutional guarantees.

Although we would not know for some time whether there would be elections, we had to move ahead on the assumption that people would be going to the polls on November 7.

At the height of the interviewing, ten were being completed each day. The interviewers would rush back to the office, find a relatively peaceful corner and begin transcribing from their tapes. They were urged to transcribe almost immediately after the interviews, first, because the meetings would still be fresh in their minds and they would be better able to decide the relative importance of certain statements; and second, with each interviewer having appointments with several legislators, the Project would be delayed if tapes were allowed to pile up. There was little danger of that, however, because of the third and most important reason for speed: we simply could not afford to buy that many tapes and had to re-use most of them.

In early August, with several interviews completed and their texts transcribed, we urgently needed a final decision on what form we wanted the profiles to take. If we did not come up with instructions for our interviewers on how we wanted the profiles prepared, we would have no uniformity in the final product.

Throughout those previous hectic months, there had been no precedents to follow for many of our problems. Many answers had come through trial and error: some things fell into place, others didn't. But fortunately the creation of a profile outline and "model" for researchers to use in writing their first drafts did not cause much trouble. The interview questionnaire itself translated into a readable and interesting profile, beginning with the legislator's service to constituents, proceeding to his view of the institution and then to his opinions on specific issues in the consumer, environmental, fiscal, transportation, human rights and labor areas. We also decided to devise an "Introduction" to each profile in order to give the reader a quick overview of that particular legislator.

Once our Project was under way, we did not follow the Congress Project methods very much because theirs was more a study of the institution itself. Moreover, we were striving for and were able to achieve much more uniformity in our profiles both because of the smaller size of our legislature and the fact that we had far fewer people writing profiles (roughly ten as compared to about two hundred in the Congress Project). But we did borrow some tips on profile writing which said, in part:

> You have access to quite a lot of information books, reports ... personal interviews. To keep all of this information in one profile and still retain the unity of your work, you will have to wind specific threads from beginning to end. Threads might be these recurring themes: member's background as it pervades activities and relationships with constituents; unique or original attitudes toward government ... or some key facets of his or her personality.

> *Focus: Provide transitions from paragraph to paragraph.*
> ... Readers cannot follow detail after detail without some aid from you.

> As for your choice of details, always bear in mind that your readers will share your curiosity. Many of the questions you want to ask the member are ones your reader will want to know also. Always remember you have a human being to consider and reveal to your members. Thus, use quotations, humor and details that let the reader see and hear what you observed or what your sources observed.

> Statistics, evidence, positions should be given living bodies so that readers can see, hear and feel the places, events and people in the profile. This does not mean purely impressionistic writing, but it does require finding and using details of actuality that allow readers to more nearly experience the person you are writing about.

Ralph Nader's suggestion to us throughout had been, "When you're in the stretch run, don't waste too much time sitting around and theorizing on what something should look like. Just do one from the beginning to end and it will help you decide what you want a profile to look like."

So, shortly after Debbie returned from the first interview, I took her transcription of Representative Camp's statements to a cabin in the woods to try and hammer out a draft of what a profile should look like. In a way, Camp was an easy one to do. Debbie had done a terrific job in researching his record, and articles from the smallest weekly newspapers in his area, campaign literature and numerous statements made by Camp on the floor of the House were included in the file. But even Camp, as several other legislators were presently to do, posed a problem. Our in-depth research was matched by the fact that he was a hard-working and extremely verbose individual. His computer printout sheet on floor statements stretched more than fifteen feet across the cabin floor. I crawled from one end to the other and back in astonishment. He seemed to have said something on every bill considered by the House!

I began typing at three in the afternoon. At six the next morning I had completed a seventeen-page draft on Herb Camp. Though I knew it could be better organized and perhaps shortened, we at least now had something to look at, criticize and rewrite. Later that morning copies of it were given to each of our researchers. They were asked to read it as soon as possible and suggest any changes.

By the end of the day most of them had decided that the Camp draft was too long and that I had put in too many subjective judgments. The critics were also concerned that it was too clogged up with statistics on voting, attendance, the number of floor statements and the like. It just didn't flow.

As a result, we decided to try to keep each profile to ten pages, typed double-space on legal-sized paper. We moved the "performance" section, which included mostly statistics, out of the profile and placed it at the end. And we all realized once again how important it was to produce profiles which spoke for themselves as much as possible, essays that presented the records and views of the legislators without too much opinion from us. We stressed the need for quotes: one can only read "he feels," "he believes," "he asserts" and "he contends" so much without getting bored. Unless you have superbly imaginative and talented writers—and even then it's no sure thing—that is the way most of the sentences in a profile will begin if you do not insert a healthy number of quotes. Moreover, the approach is surely more objective and accurate if you let the legislator do the talking. This did not mean we would neglect to point out what appeared to be contradictions, for example, between a legislator's firm "right to life" stand on abortion, and an accompanying solid endorsement of the death penalty for certain crimes.

Along with the Camp profile, then, we wrote an "Outline for Profiles" (see Appendix). As we were to learn as we went along, not enough emphasis had been placed on the kind of style we wanted, or on the information that was absolutely crucial. But the writers improved as their drafts were criticized and most of the drafts soon reflected similar formats and styles.

By the second week in August, our third week of interviewing, they were beginning to pile up. Getting them printed in volume was our next problem and, as it turned out, the problem of all problems for the entire study. On August 22, I stopped in to see Gilbert Kelman, publisher of the *Wallingford Post,* a small weekly newspaper. Kelman and CCAG had met in the summer of 1971 when we were exposing a substantial underassessment of property tax for International Silver, Inc. in Wallingford. Kelman had sided with us editorially. Subsequently, he had arranged for our bi-monthly newspaper, *The Network News,* to be printed at a low cost in his plant.

Whenever we had a printing problem, it was natural to call Kelman. So he wasn't surprised to see me walk into his office.

"What's new?" he asked in his usual jolly way. "How's this controversial project of yours?"

"Well, Gil," I said. "This Project's not going to do anybody any good unless we can get it printed in volume and distributed before the elections."

"How much of it is ready to go to press?" he asked.

"Not much. But I really can't answer the question until I know what the profiles have to look like before they go to a printer. Do they just have to be typed on clean copy?"

"That depends on how you want it to look, how you want to get the thing done. How does Ralph have those big reports of his run off?"

"Multi-lith. At least that's how they've done things like 'Power and Land in California,' 'Citibank' and 'The Chemical Feast' before they've come out as actual books."

Kelman was on the phone before I even finished the sentence. "Hi, George. I need a price." He looked over at me. "How many pages are these things?"

"Three to five."

"How many profiles?"

"Roughly one hundred and fifty."

"And how many copies of each?"

"About four hundred."

Kelman gulped into the phone. "Five times one-fifty times four hundred! Did you hear that, George?"

George heard, evidently paused and then gave a figure of more than three thousand dollars for the job.

Kelman was quite familiar with our always bleak financial

situation. But he asked anyway. "Can you afford that kind of money?"

"Afford it? We're $1600 in debt because we haven't been able to do any fund-raising for three months between this Project and competition from presidential candidates."

"And even if this guy did it for $3500, it would not include collating. He'd just put the pages in boxes and you'd have to worry about collating them. And you're talking about 300,000 pages!"

"We'd have to get the stuff to him all typed correctly, too, right?"

"Sure. If you count the typing, editing, collating, it's probably more like a $15,000 job than $3,000."

I felt sick to my stomach. The thought of having gathered all of this terrific information and not being able to get it out!

"Do you think we can beat this guy's price by much?" I asked Kelman.

"I don't know. He's obviously giving me a deal since I do business with him all the time. How nice do you want these things to look?"

"Better than some third-rate copier job."

"That's where you run into problems. Almost anything that looks good is going to cost you."

I told Gil Kelman thanks, I'd be in touch.

The Project was proceeding at nothing less than a furious pace by the third week in August. We had recruited five volunteer editors to rewrite and improve the first draft profiles and we were making a great many calls to different printers who had been recommended by friends as likely to give us a good deal. The more calls we made, the more depressing it became. Excluding typing and collating, the prices were six thousand dollars and up.

Some people had suggested a regular book publisher

might be interested, but the two we visited were unable or unwilling to handle it. We tried one more printer who told us that "anything under $5000 would be a bargain."

The next week put us into September. To be very honest, we were by then at least privately hoping the elections would be postponed until January, mainly because that would give us time to raise some money. We were broke and it was only an "emergency grant" from Ralph that allowed us to stay in operation. This was something that neither we nor Ralph had wanted to happen. Our Connecticut model had been founded on the assumption that the nation's richest state would be able to find enough citizen support to maintain the group. But the presidential campaign, and especially the McGovern campaign, along with our own inability to find any time to solicit funds made it necessary to seek Ralph's financial support on a one-shot basis at this point.

That week the Superior Court in Hartford handed down a decision mandating state legislative elections in November and, even though the Democrats appealed immediately, there was little hope the decision would be overturned. Upon hearing of the court ruling, I raced into the back room where Marty was busy typing.

"We're in trouble," I said. "I just don't see any way that we're going to get this stuff printed and out to constituents."

"Maybe we'd better go see Gil," said Marty.

But it appeared that if we wanted someone to type, print and collate the profiles we might have to spend well over ten thousand dollars. The three of us moaned about the possibility of the whole summer's work going down the drain.

"Well, gentlemen," said Gil. "I see only one way out," his face contorted, his expression somewhere between a smirk and a grin.

Marty caught on before I did. "Oh, no. No. NO! Absolutely not, Gil. We are not going to print this whole goddam thing ourselves."

Gil Kelman threw his hands up in the air. "So how else are you going to get it done? It's like most other things you people have done in the past year—you've done them yourselves."

"I can't believe you're serious," I ranted. "We'd never be able to do it. We don't have the equipment."

"Rent typewriters and a couple more mimeograph machines," Gil suggested. He was the only calm person in the room.

"This is all we need," moaned Marty. "Our people are at the ends of their ropes as it is. They've been thinking they're almost done with this thing."

"Yes, but if it's a matter of getting it done or not getting it done, we might not have any choice."

By ten o'clock that evening we were back at the office, breaking the news to the staff. Most of them just looked at us as though the long hot furious summer had finally taken its toll; we had flipped our lids. A couple of people, I found out later, were really quite upset. With most of the researchers either gone or on their way out—most of them to return to school—Debbie and Emily knew that the real burden would fall on them. Debbie must have been regretting her talks to administrators at Smith College who permitted her to spend the fall term at CCAG full-time.

"I had planned on spending a great deal of time on energy matters," Debbie recalls. "During the spring, I had only really gotten my feet wet. But when I discovered that we were going to produce this massive amount of material and see that it was distributed, I could see my energy study fading away."

Emily had not planned on staying into the fall. She had

graduated from college the previous spring and had been looking forward to traveling and either a job or graduate school. "It was really distasteful, not the thought of staying longer—I loved the organization and the people—but it was the idea of doing more drudgery to get the study out."

Fortunately both Debbie and Emily shared something with the rest of us, permanent CCAG people. Worse than the thought of producing the material ourselves, of mimeographing, proofreading, collating and all the other menial tasks involved, was the notion that if we did not do it, the whole Project would have been in vain.

It turned out to be a pretty simple matter after the initial shock wore off, however. Here was this tremendous information and we knew there had never been anything like it done on a state legislature. And here was a need to mass produce it and get it out. Our task was pretty well defined. The only thing that could stand in the way was our own reluctance.

We dove into the task. The next morning Marty was on the phone trying to find six typewriters. We had decided the night before, with Gil Kelman's help, that the best looking profile would be one typed on legal-size paper sideways in two columns. Only certain kinds of typewriters would take those fourteen inches of paper. And we were in heavy competition with political campaign headquarters at all levels which had gobbled up most of the typewriters not only in Hartford, but in most other Connecticut cities as well. We finally located one company that rented us three machines and nearly a week later we got our hands on three more. Finding the two additional mimeograph machines to join the one we had been using for more than a year was not quite as difficult.

If the prospect of having to type all those profiles was discouraging, it was even worse to think that they all had to be typed on stencils. Although we liked to rely on volunteers as much as possible, this was a time when we had to be honest enough with ourselves to admit that something we wanted had to be bought. If we had waited for volunteer typists, we might still be there with all those unprinted profiles.

With machines in place, we began taking calls from people who had seen our ads in the major daily newspapers. No one who typed less than fifty words per minute would be hired. Since it seemed to us that a good typist could complete three stencils in an hour, we offered one dollar per stencil.

Work was available just about whenever anyone wanted it. Some applicants were former secretaries who now had grown children. Others had jobs during the day and were looking for a little extra money at night.

Our turnover rate was very high, especially in the beginning. Some people answered the ad apparently thinking they would be working in a luxurious office. Upon arriving and seeing our offices, several just turned around and left. After a summer of research, tape transcribing and profile-writing in every conceivable part of the offices, which covered most of the second floor, the place was not as neat as it might have been. But even though we tried to clean up the large rooms in which the typists would be working, they remained dirty. Great amounts of dust—or maybe it was soot—seemed to land on everything. Other applicants became discouraged at the prospect of typing stencils.

But some of the typists just couldn't type very well, even after we gave them a period to adjust to the stencils. Day after day we would introduce new people to the process, sit them down at a typewriter and an hour or so later hear the agonizingly slow, unrhythmic sound of the machine. Tap . . . . . tap . . . . . tap . . . tap . . . tap . tap . tap.

Once the typing procedure settled down to a semblance of routine, a problem developed with the editing. The tendency to take an area or segment of the Project for granted came back to haunt us again. None of us had thought too much about how the first drafts would be edited. We knew that we had some people who said they would be happy to help with editing, but we didn't realize the degree of guidance they would need.

Finding that some editors were merely correcting grammatical mistakes when what we really needed was a critical review of the profile, we prepared some "Guidelines for Profile Editors." After giving each editor a brief description of the Project and its goals, these guidelines listed fifteen instructions to be followed when addressing a drafted profile. Among our suggestions were:

1. Try to eliminate value judgments that seem unsubstantiated. Either find quotes or data in the file to support them and add that information in, or eliminate the conclusion altogether.

2. Pull colorful quotes or important stated positions of the legislator and elevate them to the beginnings of sections.

3. Try to present any major contradictions in positions, but do it in a way which eliminates your having to call the legislator a hypocrite.

4. For a committee chairman, try to insert as much information as possible about how the person has handled the leadership position.

5. VERY IMPORTANT: In the Service to Constituents section, eliminate adjectives describing the member unless you can describe at least generally who said them (i.e. "a businessman said" or "an environmental advocate said"). Don't simply say, "Rep. Jones' constituents describe him as insensitive."

In some cases the editors actually became profile writters. Some of the people who had only been with us for the summer had left their transcribed interviews and the files of their legislators without having completed their first draft profiles. This only occurred in a few cases, but where it did we had to have profiles drafted by people who had not taken part in the research. Fortunately in most of these situations we had also asked the researchers to make tapes of their impressions and listening to these usually helped the stand-in profile writers.

There were other editing problems, too. Some of the drafted profiles were incredibly boring. In some cases, it was because a researcher had not used enough quotes or taken enough from the file, but other legislators were just impossible to spruce up. Another problem was length. As the production process appeared more and more massive and complicated, we urged that the length be kept under ten pages. In some cases it was not difficult, but in others it was next to impossible.

It took John Wancheck longer than most to complete his first profile, but when he delivered it to us it was obvious why. It measured nearly twenty legal-sized pages. When we told him that it would have to be cut, he managed a sick grin. "How can you do that to my masterpiece?"

Some of the staff argued that we needed more editors, but I was stubborn about using no more than six. "This is the one place where we need control and uniformity," I kept saying. And I insisted as well on reading every profile before it was viewed by the legislators and typed on stencil. Ultimately one person had to be responsible for the contents, and it made sense that it should be the Director. Besides, in the event that I was questioned by a reporter on the contents of a profile, I wanted to be totally familiar with it.

It was convenient that all of our editors lived in the

Hartford area, but when we were offered help from a friend in New York City who had extensive experience, we could not afford to turn her down. She edited about twenty profiles, and did it well, in the time that the rest of us were working on three or four.

We felt that the finished product had to be available to the public at least two weeks before the election on November 7, and a specific date had to be set soon for their release.

The profiles were not the type of material that could simply be delivered to the press without warning. We needed time to investigate possible distribution outlets—bookstores, libraries, business offices, etc.

But before any release date could be set, there had to be an assessment—an honest one—of what was left to do and how long it would take to do it.

The mimeo machines could go almost around the clock; by that first week in October, they were turning out several thousand sheets an hour. To assist Debbie and Emily on the machines, we had hired two other people, one the wife of the head of Connecticut's lettuce boycott, the other a guy who had simply walked in and asked if he could help. (He looked very much like Jesus Christ but did not work with as much dedication.)

Supplies were somewhat of a problem. It seemed that we ordered another hundred thousand sheets of mimeo paper almost daily. Suppliers could not always give such large quantities of paper when we needed it or they would make it available at a warehouse so that we would have to take a van and pick it up ourselves. Neighbors on our block grew accustomed to seeing us unloading the van and carrying box after box up the steep stairway to our offices.

Likewise with the mimeo machines. The storeowner from

whom we bought ink was astounded to see us return time after time, and each time something went wrong with one of the machines, we attempted to fix it ourselves. Our people became pretty fair mechanics. But we did have a service contract for the mimeo machines and had several visits from servicemen from the owner's store. At one point he called us and said, "I've never had such an experience. What are you doing with those machines anyway, running them around the clock?"

He was not far off. We were doing at least fifteen hours a day and were willing to go twenty-four hours if necessary. But the more crucial problem now became getting those materials collated. We had expected to collate all of the individual profiles ourselves between our own staff and volunteers. A huge table had been assembled from a thick piece of lumber and cinder blocks. This "collating room" was located in the very rear of our second-floor offices, directly behind the mimeograph machines. As the profile pages came off the machines, people went to work on them.

We called friends and asked them to come by and help. Some of them did, but not on any full-time basis. So we played an avalanche of Public Service Announcements on the radio pleading for volunteers. The local FM rock station, a good friend of ours, was so concerned that we might not complete the Project that he began running the announcements nearly every fifteen minutes during our peak production period. It was not unusual to tune in to the station at two or three in the morning and hear:

> Listen here now. The folks over at CCAG are at it again tonight, making up those profiles on your state legislators. This is a project for the people. Why not drop over there to 57 Farmington Avenue and give them a hand.

We had a few people come in at those hours, but in most cases people who were up at three in the morning evidently were enjoying what they were doing and didn't bother to drop over.

Something had to be done about collating. It was taking too many people and too long. Although we had received few donations of any kind during the summer, we were now bailed out by the businessman-father of one of our workers. Interested in donating something to a rehabilitation center in Hartford, he suggested that we truck our uncollated profiles to the center and he would pay the patients there to do the work. The center was a big place where they could string several long tables together and the collaters could simply walk around them gathering the sheets.

The next possible obstacle to having the profiles out in time was typing. Our faithful typists were still plugging away, producing about eight profiles on stencil a day. But our projections showed that their pace might not allow us to meet our goal. So we added one more typist and Portia Iverson, who had just finished her editing, moved to one of the typewriters.

Now we could set a date for release of the profiles. Since Nader's Congress Project was to be released on Sunday, October 22, 1972 (with press conferences in Hartford and several other eastern cities), we chose to release ours two days later on the 24th.

The production went forward. We had attorneys repairing typewriters and mimeograph machines, transportation specialists collating, and Marty arrived at 8:30 every Sunday morning to open the office door for our weekend typing crew. Even our friends asked if we were out of our minds. "What was the summer like?" we would ask them. All we knew was it had been very hot, in many ways.

By the second week in October, there was little space left in our offices. We had purchased large used boxes and placed profiles in them; at least three hundred collated, stapled profiles ready to be distributed and another two hundred held together with paper clips. Those boxes were everywhere and on them were scrawled the names of the legislators whose profiles they contained.

Whether or not we would be able to produce bound volumes as well as the individual profiles by election time was questionable. Our primary goal was the individual profiles, but it would be necessary to provide reporters with profiles on every legislator anyway, so it made sense to find a way to get the volumes bound.

After several days of searching, we found a man who said he could produce covers that would serve our purpose of holding the profiles together and would also look attractive. But was there time? He wanted to know if we could give him the design for the cover all ready and prepared for printing.

Lying around our office had been an excellent photograph taken by Tom Zetterstrom, our volunteer cameraman. It showed the State Capitol and the sidewalk leading up to it. On the sidewalk were footprints (Tom had made them by getting his feet muddy and then trudging along the walk). They could be interpreted as citizen steps, a good sign that the public was becoming more involved in the legislature. Or they could be the steps of special interest lobbyists who had always dominated state capitols. No matter how you read it, it was a good picture. Another volunteer expert, Frank Von Holtshausen, designed the cover on silk-screen using Tom's photograph.

The design was then sent to Utica, New York, where more than two hundred covers were made, with the picture and the name of our group on the front and the back plain. They were done in dark blue with the drawing and lettering in white and came back to us in eight days with three holes punched in them along one edge. The fellow who had sold them to us suggested we contact a local company with the equipment to punch three corresponding holes in the profiles we planned to bind.

But before they could punch those holes, the profiles had to be put together into volumes. That meant collating more than two hundred copies of the volume—each with a total of nearly 1300 pages. It was yet another major task to anticipate once we finally completed the individual profiles.

On the morning of October 18, I raced into the office with a copy of the Introduction, typed on stencil and ready to be mimeographed. While it was going through the machines, we discussed how we would collate the profiles for the bound volume. I had promised that we would deliver them the next morning for hole-punching. One of our problems now was that we had gone through so many crises we began to think we could do just about anything: completing this task in one evening just did not seem like that much of a problem.

By this time all of the individual profiles had been collated and were stacked throughout our office. Our plan was to separate the legislators into sections and alphabetize them within each: the House rank and file members would be done first (so they would appear at the back of the book), then the House leadership. The same process would be repeated for the Senate and an explanation of the bills and the Introduction added last. We started at the end of the alphabet in the House member section and planned to place as many copies of each person's profile as we could in the hallways of the second and third floors. All of this would begin after the offices upstairs, occupied by an advertising agency, were vacated for the evening. This would then be repeated for each legislator until we reached the beginning of the alphabet and the Introduction. At that point we would have as many completed volumes as could fit in the hall-ways.

As it turned out, that number was less than seventy. And it took us all night to complete just that many. That night was probably the worst of the entire Project from a work standpoint. A few people had to be forced to go home. We finished about six A.M. but were, by that time, in a semi-trance. At seven, the van was loaded with the collated profiles, each volume wrapped in brown paper. We drove them the twelve miles to be punched.

Those first volumes were to be ready by mid-afternoon. After a few hours sleep, we met again, all of us agreeing that there had to be a better way to collate the remaining two-thirds of the profiles. We decided to use as many tables as we could find, place the profiles on them in order, and have our people walk around gathering them into volumes. This system could be no worse than the one used the night before.

I think the most pleasant moment of all those months was clamping the cover on to the first volume. We had been provided with special four-inch screw-posts that fit nicely through the holes punched in the covers and in the profiles.

With seven bound volumes, I headed immediately for New York, planning to stop in Westport to deliver the first one to a *New York Times* reporter. We felt it was important to allow the press to have bound volumes before the week-end, so they would really have a chance to go through it.

The rest of the staff prepared for another long evening of collating and additional volunteers were brought in. But the anticipated trauma never developed. The new system was immensely better than the old and all of the collating was completed by a little after midnight.

Like the initial research period in June, the production process had been a real test. All of us had worked incredibly long hours in the latter phase and had suffered through many more obstacles. But by the time production started we knew we had something good and valuable: we knew that this material was going to be released. While we had no illusions about its turning around the state legislative elections as a whole, we knew it would have an impact.

The Profiles
Go Public

WE HAD DEVELOPED a "new product," manufactured it and were now faced with the most essential aspect of any business—letting people know that the product existed, making them eager to own it and getting it into their hands.

Unfortunately, we had no advertising budget; we could not hire high-priced ad firms or purchase space and time in the media to tout our profiles as "the one, the only, the original!" (which they were), or exhort people to be "the first on your block to read about. . . ."

The answer to this, of course, was publicity—creating and generating coverage that would place our product on the news pages free and prominently.

The press seemed to have forgotten about the Project since our last state-wide coverage on the preparations for interviews in late July. During the interim (it was now early October), we had been too busy to seek out publicity and, to be honest, we had not been terribly newsworthy. The only headline we could possibly have generated in that time would have read:

CCAG Worker Yawns 345 Times While Researching Legislative Floor Statements.

But now we had a seven-and-a-half-pound, 1300-page report, the most carefully researched document on the General Assembly ever produced and this, we felt, was NEWS.

Yet, how would an editor feel about us if we dumped this tome into his lap on the day we scheduled it for release? Negatively, to say the least, and not without justification. How unfair it would be to an editor, and to us, if we allowed only a few hours for analysis of the material.

Our release date of October 24 had been carefully chosen for reasons of, among other things, competition for newspaper space and radio and TV time. There would be no major campaign speeches and few visiting firemen scheduled. It would be two days after the Congress Project was released, which would make us a natural part of the continuing story of legislative studies. But our greatest fear was that the Vietnam War would end on the same day our profiles were released. (It was being hinted at as imminent by the Administration.) Oh, we wanted peace as desperately as anyone, but not on that day, please.

Well in advance of October 24, then, we lined up key news people, offering advance stories to whet the appetite of the public. Two of the most prominent people responded immediately.

I called Don Noel who handles the editorial page for the *Hartford Times* and who had written pro-CCAG editorials on a couple of occasions. Noel could not be considered an automatic supporter, however: he is an intellectual who studies his subjects carefully and has been known to write editorials damning or severely criticizing a position or issue that he, as a "liberal," might be expected to support.

Noel had more of a stake in the Project than most other newsmen. When we had originally announced the effort in May, he had written a glowing editorial which urged public support for it and our fund-raising efforts.

When Noel came by, Marty, Angie and I made sure we were available. First Angie described how we had carried out the research at the Capitol. Noel, a strong supporter of the public's right to know and defender of Freedom of Information statutes, was especially interested in the obstacles that confronted us in attempting to gain access to legislative records, particularly committee transcripts.

We showed him what our file of an individual legislator looked like. "Where did you find these computer printouts on floor debates?" he asked, gazing approvingly at the form. When we told him, his eyes lit up.

While we talked in Angie's office, the mimeograph machines were banging away in the large adjoining room. From time to time, Marty would have to excuse himself to make a repair on one of them.

We showed Don Noel some of the profiles that had already come off the presses and been collated and stapled. He asked, "How will these be distributed? How many of each profile are you making up? Do you think that the public will buy them?"

Noel left without promising anything.

The next day we had a similar meeting with Don Meikle, then Capitol reporter for Associated Press. Like Noel, Meikle had not been a visitor to our office before. He had written a couple of stories about the Project while it was going on, one on the outspoken man who threw his questionnaire in the wastebasket, another on legislators' responses to our questionnaire seeking financial information. So, as with Noel, it was reasonable to expect that he might want to do an advance story.

Meikle could not hide his enthusiasm as well as Noel had. As we gave him a tour through the second floor, past box after box with legislators' names scrawled on the outside and hundreds of profiles on the inside, he flashed a wide grin and kept saying, "I can't believe it. I can't believe it! I can't believe you've done all this work!"

When Meikle left the office that day, all of us were convinced that he was going to race back to his typewriter and bang out a story about a fantastic citizen-produced study that was about to be released. He came through with not only one article but with a whole series.

We attempted to drum up interest in advance stories with several other daily newspapers, too. Getting news people into the office and giving them an idea of the kind of production job that was involved was crucial. But we were unable to attract any others. Some editors simply could not grasp the enormity of the material. They were more concerned with adequately covering everyday "hard news."

We turned our attention to television and WTIC, the state's largest station, jumped at the opportunity. In a meeting with the news director and his assistant I presented samples of some of the information that was to be released one week hence. We also provided copies of the Nader reports well in advance and kept them informed on Nader's Hartford press conference.

Following the Nader conference, a WTIC newsman conducted an interview with some of us which was used on the newscasts during the weekend, and this helped us achieve our purpose of "advancing" our release.

I cannot overestimate the importance of discussing a project of this magnitude with news editors well in advance of its release. Permitting them time to digest the material is one reason. But also important is the necessity to alert them beforehand so that they can advise their suburban "stringers" of the situation. Daily newspapers have, in most cases, several different editions, and with the increasing growth of the suburbs, they concentrate more and more on these suburban editions. "Stringers," reporters who file stories exclusively about their immediate localities—sewer pipe installations on Country Road, a request for zoning variance to build a porch, or the PTA meeting at Honeyhill School—would not ordinarily be aware of the big picture, or how the legislative profiles, in this case, would interest their readers. Generally, as part-time reporters, stringers do not seek out a story, and so they must be contacted in advance by their editors when one arises in their province.

As so many of the profiles were on legislators who represent suburban areas, it was vital to have this coverage.

I might also add something about a situation which may confront others who plan this sort of project. We discovered that the farther we got from Hartford, the heart of the matter, the less interest the press had in the story. This was most evident in Lower Fairfield County; an area that lies heavily under the influence of New York City; an area from which commuters depart each morning to make their livings in The City; an area where *The New York Times* and New York television dominate news sources. The residents may be aware of activities in Albany, but rarely in Hartford. The dailies here provide perfunctory coverage of the state legislature, if they provide any at all.

"What goes on in Hartford has nothing to do with us," said one of the area editors.

In his editorial "Audacity and Hard Work for Public Information," printed just before our profiles were released to the public, Don Noel concluded with the following story:

There's an interesting little gentleman's wager between Toby

Moffett, Director of CCAG, and Marty Rogol, one of the two attorneys on the scantily-paid staff who was doubling as a mimeograph turner the afternoon I dropped in. The pessimistic side of the bet is that most copies (of the 300 or so available for each district) will be left over. The optimistic side is that most will be gone within a week. I hope the optimist wins. If there are not in every legislative district in this State 300 people who really care what their elected representatives have been up to, it won't say much for the quality of Nutmeg citizenry.

Unfortunately, it wasn't as simple as that. Getting the material into the hands of the people is extremely difficult, even when you have the time, money and expertise in distribution methods. We had none of those. Our attempts to create a distribution system came far too late in the Project. It wasn't until about a week before we released the profiles that one person began working full-time on it. Actually we should have put someone to work on it in the middle of the summer. But we could never seem to find that extra person.

We had two different situations for distribution: there were the bound copies, containing each and every profile for the entire General Assembly, and there were individual legislator profiles, 300 copies for each district.

We had decided to charge a dollar for each profile, not a bad buy for a document that contained an average of ten pages of facts on a legislator's record and statements by him on crucial issues. For the complete bound volume, we came up with a sliding scale of prices: $25 for individual citizens, civic groups, libraries and schools; $50 for state-wide labor unions and state agencies; and $100 for corporations and lobbyists for profit-making corporations.

Would corporations pay one hundred dollars for a report

from a citizen group which most of them viewed as an adversary? We weren't sure, but we felt our price was reasonable.

The corporations' responses proved us right. A few days after the study was released I spoke before the Harvard Club of Hartford. Following my talk, which had been dominated by a discussion of the General Assembly Project, an insurance company executive rushed up to me. "I've got to have a copy of it, right away," he said. An insurance lobbyist also ordered a copy of the bound volume, writing a check for a hundred dollars on the spot. "He usually spends more than that on lunch," a friend remarked.

Several times during the following weeks and months, when corporate representatives approached us for copies of the bound volume, we asked them, "How much would it have cost you to produce this report?" Based on the number of hours per week their people work and their salaries, answers ranged from $75,000 to $200,000. A hundred dollars was a bargain.

Getting the bound volumes into other institutions was not as easy. But once we developed a plan of action, distribution was simple. A couple of our staff members spent the last three weeks before the election phoning libraries, schools and other groups to try to sell the volumes. A large number of libraries both in and out of the state placed orders. For most of them we delivered the books; others were asked for five dollars extra to cover the cost of mailing the seven-and-a-half-pound report.

But getting the individual profiles out was something else again. We began with our core of thirty or so Citizens' Lobby co-ordinators around the state—a built-in distribution system. We also sent them profiles of the individual legislators for their lobbyists, if those legislators were seeking re-election. Some of those CCAG lobbyists took profiles in larger quantities and sold them to other people in their towns.

Where our lobby was not particularly strong, we sought out civic organizations or citizens who may have contacted us with offers of help at one time or another. This helped us get profiles around, but usually only five or ten at a time.

We also contacted bookstores throughout the state. Most of them agreed to take about fifty profiles and sell them for the dollar we requested. A few wanted a percentage of the sale price and we agreed to it. In fact, in any situation where there was a problem with prices, we gave in. If people were reluctant to make a donation for the profiles, we simply gave them away, feeling it was more important to get the information out than to make money to cover our expenses.

The profiles would have sold better, of course, if our distribution had been better, and if there had been time to generate more publicity in every newspaper in the state. But while several dailies and a few weeklies used the profiles extensively, over a period of several days or weeks, most simply covered the initial release.

In some bookstores the profiles sold very well, while in others they did not. We learned from various people that the volume did not stand out enough as a sales display to make people notice the material at a glance. But once a person actually began to read the profile on his or her legislator, we were told, the material would not be put down until completed.

We believed so strongly in the value of the profiles that a week before the elections we planned a campaign to hand them out in shopping centers, outside major corporations and other places where mass distribution was possible. This decision was reached with considerable controversy among the staff. "Haven't we learned by now that when you give people something for nothing, they'll continue to take you for granted?" somebody asked, referring to our history of having mailed materials to individuals over the course of the past year and receiving no donations from most of them during our fund-raising campaigns.

There is indeed a problem with giving things away, even when you ask the people, as we did, to send a dollar if they liked the profiles.

We then found that we could disseminate the information in the profiles without actually placing the material in the hands of the public by appearing on radio talk shows where the listening audience phones in questions. As we discussed the Project, the phone lines lit up.

"I want to know how Buckley voted on abortion."

"What does Sullivan say about the income tax?"

"Is DeNardis for mass transportation?"

Many of the callers would start by asking general questions like, "What do you think of Representative Dice?" In those instances, we would either ask for a more specific question or read some of the factual highlights from the profile.

On WELI in New Haven, we had five phones lit up for two hours straight. Near the end of the program, people were calling in and asking if the program would be on again. After all, they said, we haven't talked about *all* the New Haven area representatives. The host, John Bouchard, said that if I were willing to come back, he would check with the station management about the possibility of a special show. Four days later, a special two-hour Sunday evening program was aired. It was just two days before the election and people responded even more enthusiastically than they had on the first show. Apathy? Lack of interest? These people are desperate for this information, I remember thinking then. Even if they want it delivered over their radio which saves them the trouble of having to read the whole thing.

But there were callers who said they wanted to read about it, too. Some asked where they could buy the entire volume on their legislators. Many more asked another question: "Why haven't we read about this in the *New Haven Register*?"

The *New Haven Register* is the major daily in that area. For years it has directed severe criticism at the General Assembly, some of it based on issues and evidence, some of it merely rhetoric. On the day our profiles were released, the *Register* had run a front-page story, the bulk of it on how New Haven area legislators had responded to questions about the media. It was a paranoid approach. Here is a paper that is known as an adversary of the legislature. It is a paper that is disliked by area legislators as carping and uncooperative. Now, a report comes out providing page after page of substantive information about those legislators' records and points of view. Yet, of a forty-two page questionnaire, the paper emphasized one question—about its own coverage!

When those callers asked, "Why hasn't this been in the *Register*?" I merely said that I really didn't know. "Several other papers around the state have been running entire profiles or excerpts from them all during the past week," I replied. "They feel that the profiles will serve as an aid to voters, since there is so little other information available to them on their state representatives." I suggested that they might better find out by calling the editors of the *Register* themselves.

Publicly criticizing specific newspapers or other media does not usually work to the advantage of citizen groups, especially if you're trying to operate—and get coverage—in a one-newspaper town. During our first year we had adhered to that philosophy with only one exception, when one of our attorneys had served as counsel to a Hartford coalition challenging the license renewal of the state's largest TV station. But in almost all instances when we had gripes about media coverage, of us or any other group or event, we went privately to the editors or publishers. Those conferences usually helped at least temporarily to improve the coverage, partly because we were persuasive and probably partly because of the implicit threat of our launching a public campaign on the issue.

On the WELI show I had no intention of going after the *Register*. Whether some of those WELI callers contacted the *Register* as I suggested, or whether the *Register* management heard the show, the paper interpreted my remarks—or wanted to—as a declaration of war.

A Sunday column which ran from the top to the bottom of a page took aim at "Toby Moffett's complaints:"

We think we gave the CCAG General Assembly project the news space it deserved in New Haven newspapers. What may have been done in Hartford, where the State Capitol and both houses of the General Assembly are, in essence, a "local industry" with many resident employes, or in New London where there may have been other good reasons for more detailed reports, are comparisons not particularly relevant to sound New Haven news coverage.

One of the ironies of the Connecticut Citizens Action Group's persistent eagerness to take pot-shots at the press by quoting sour grapes from members of the General Assembly is the fact that lawmakers are habitually petulant with a press that puts them on the spot. They love and endorse a press that praises them. The biggest gripe against our New Haven newspapers is the fact that we defended the taxpayer's interest (much as

CCAG sets out to defend the consumer interest) against a half-baked income tax proposition that caught many lawmakers voting "Yes" one month and "No" the next in the summer of 1971.

At any rate, we think we did right by CCAG in our reporting even if we did not meet the group's expectations publicity-wise. One of the first rules of consumer-interest, or public-interest, activity is to look beyond the packaging to examine the content of a product. In this case, and in our opinion, a very big CCAG package in terms of size had less impact in terms of content— news content, that is. And news—fairly, accurately, and more or less concisely presented—is what a newspaper is about.

I refuted this article, point by point, in a long statement to the paper, stating that I thought they had missed the entire point of the Project and seemed unaware of the individual profiles and their value. It was never printed.

After the election, there was very little coverage. From time to time during the ensuing months, the profiles would be mentioned in legislative stories or editorially, always in a favorable light. As with press coverage throughout the Project, it was necessary, in most cases, to generate stories ourselves, to make suggestions to editors and reporters for possible articles or "angles." When a particular issue was in the news, utility rates for example, it was important to phone reporters who covered that story and mention the stands that certain key legislators had taken during our study, or feed the reporters a simple statistic, such as the percentage of legislators who said we need tougher utility regulation. These are the little things that count in dealing with the press and how we have since been able to insure fairly steady publicity.

The Light at the End of the Tunnel

DID IT WORK? Did the Project help the good guys win and the not-so-good guys be defeated? Let's put it this way without meaning to hedge: if this had not been a national election year, the results might have been more clear-cut.

In any year, the impact of the profiles on the elections would be difficult to measure. But in 1972, an evaluation was almost impossible. The Nixon sweep made it an abnormal year politically. Democrats in heavily Democratic districts suddenly found their registration margin evaporated and Republicans running as sacrificial lambs against supposedly heavy odds became the favorites in their races with barely lifting a finger.

We had our own particular Connecticut problems as well. The redistricting hassle had left voters confused about state legislative races. Many simply pulled the party lever or only voted for national office candidates. Others in large numbers failed to show up at the polls at all.

Added to these problems were our shortcomings in distribution of the profiles. What little analysis of our election impact is possible shows that where our profiles were well distributed in a district, they had an effect.

In one heavily Democratic, working class city, the local weekly newspaper printed the profile of the powerful Democratic Senator who had told one of our interviewers, "You have no right to be doing this. Support of incumbents would be more in the public interest." The Nixon sweep notwithstanding, there was little else to explain his subsequent defeat except the wide publicity given his profile. His constituents were also alerted about his record through a popular talk show on which I was a guest. Since then, the man who defeated him has frequently told us how much the profile helped—and how anxious he, the new Representative, is to have a record which will result in a favorable profile when we do our next Project.

Another Representative places almost all credit for his narrow victory on our profile of him. No matter how one views his record, he had shown himself to be conscientious and aggressive, and his profile reflected this. Through a local consumer group, the document was widely distributed in the community and although Nixon captured his town by a wide margin, this Democrat survived.

There were several examples of Republicans in heavily Republican districts favored to win handily whether there had been a Nixon landslide or not, who posted only the narrowest of margins. In one small town, Nixon chalked up a six-to-one edge, but the incumbent legislator from there, one of the eighteen who had refused to cooperate with us and who had a passive and unresponsive record, won by only forty votes out of several hundred cast.

The influence of the profiles on the electorate may have been somewhat spotty, but their influence on the legislators themselves was significant. Our efforts had made it very clear that the CCAG was here to stay, and that "little brother" would be watching—even when no political campaigns were in progress (which is most of the time).

When the Senate leaders pledged at the beginning of the legislative session that all committee meetings would be open to the public, we felt the action was partly attributable to our mention of "secret" committee meetings. To make sure the pledge was honored, we formed a coalition with other citizen groups, taking turns covering these meetings and keeping them public.

In the past year, we have received calls for assistance on numerous bills from legislators who deeply felt the need for more information—or at least information from a source other than industrial lobbyists.

The chairman of an important Senate committee reacted to our strong criticism of a bill at a public hearing by asking us to draft amendments, and he subsequently incorporated these into his version of the bill.

Best of all, our relationship with many legislative staff members has improved to the point where we have been asked to act as partners in drafting several bills.

And even though the election results did not reflect a tremendous impact by our Project, we have discovered that the citizens are becoming aware of our work; we have become a clearinghouse for legislative matters, answering inquiries about bills and informing interested citizens of the best strategy for influencing certain legislation.

"How could you possibly know so much about all these legislators?" asked one woman who had just received a briefing on lobbying strategy for child protection bills she was interested in supporting. Angie pointed to a copy of our Project.

The services we have been performing have not been

limited to what might be considered our friends and allies. Representatives of small businesses have contacted us for instructions and advice. At times this has surprised us and, truthfully, made us reluctant to offer help in a few cases where we knew that we would be aiding the "opposition" on a given bill. But our public offer to supply anyone with information, to offer the results of our Project to any group or individual, has to be honored.

With almost ten speaking engagements a week among the staff, we have the opportunity to gauge public reaction to our work. More often than not we are addressing a Rotary or Kiwanis or Women's Club rather than another consumer group.

At the Colchester Rotary Club dinner in March, 1973, I had not yet finished talking about the General Assembly Project when a man in the rear of the room rose and said, "This stuff is important to history. I move we purchase a copy for the town." Informed that the town library already had a copy, he answered, "I don't give a damn. We can use more than one."

Though our problems with distribution convinced us that it takes a long time for this kind of information to sift down into the communities, we had no real idea of how long it takes. Even several months after releasing the profiles, with the excitement of elections over, we found that people are still discovering the profiles and ordering copies of them. Our supply of the bound volume has sold out and, while we do have some of the individual profiles left, we have the feeling that the 1974 edition of the Project may become a best seller.

I can't think of any other way we could have gained so much credibility with such a wide range of citizens than through the Project. In a real sense, this Project knew no politics. The VFW people, the taxpayers' associations, consumer groups, farmers, they all used the material. An insurance or banking lobbyist with a copy under his arm at the State Capitol is even now a common sight.

However, the ideal situation would be to have this kind of project carried out by citizens themselves in local communities. They could do the groundwork, the newspaper research and community leader interviews, perhaps sending the gathered material to a central staff for compilation. For them, and others, I offer the following recommendations, based on the Project experiences of the CCAG.

1. Don't sensationalize your project. Our initial mistake was to make too much of an issue over conflicts of interest. This not only alienated many legistors, but also caused the press to focus on one portion of the study when others were more important.

2. Keep the project non-partisan both in appearance and practice.

3. When you have limited time and resources, use them to draft profiles rather than write "white papers" on pet legislative topics.

4. Organize the project to coincide with elections. This will insure your visibility and improve your chances for impact, and citizens will welcome the information you provide.

5. Create an efficient, imaginative and continuing press operation, cultivate editors and reporters and find volunteers who can write clear, clean copy.

6. Use volunteers wherever possible. Tell them what the "big picture" is and utilize their special talents. If they have no expertise, set up the organization so that you know where they can fit in. (Most people, we have found, have *some* talents.)

7. Keep a continuous file on voting records and other research so that it will not pile up and overburden the staff.

8. Include other groups in the project, not necessarily to run it, but to participate in developing the important areas that must be covered in interviews with legislators. Concentrate on groups that have a record of interest in legislative matters, if possible.

9. Where possible, involve unaffiliated constituents in the project.

10. Tape record when you interview.

11. Plan and establish a production system and a good method of distribution EARLY in the project.

12. Make your project a continuing one. If your group is not sure it can do this, at least give the impression that you are. You'd be surprised how even the "possibility" of a repeat performance will change legislative behavior.

The important point is to get into the habit of looking over legislative shoulders. Regardless of who is in office, the monitoring is vital.

How are citizens involved in this often dreary effort, especially when there is no campaign in progress? The answer is to organize people around their needs—around a local property tax fight, against lax pollution control, for an improved school curriculum—and mold that group into permanency that can move on to wider, needier fields.

Timing is all. For those groups who plan to follow our lead, I know the results will be measurable as well as immeasurable. They will start earlier, they will know about production, distribution and publicity—all those things we had to learn about through trial and error and, of course, they can always turn to us.

Eventually, perhaps, state government will become everybody's business.

Epilogue

ALMOST EXACTLY one year after launching the General Assembly Project, CCAG has not stopped churning out information and materials on important issues. Having spent so many months in concentrated thought and effort on one idea during the Project, we have now returned to the basic concept of consumer and citizen action in other fields, such as the environment, human rights and consumer issues.

In New Haven we are being sued by pharmacists for conducting a survey of prescription drug prices in fifty-six New Haven area stores. Our study has shown not only wide discrepancies among stores for the same item, but also different prices being quoted to different people for the same prescription in the same store. Moreover, we have found pharmacists attempting to bargain with surveyors once they guessed that a survey was being conducted.

Our fifty-page report on the sorry record of the Occupational Health unit within the Department of Health was almost the only source of information referred to by both House and Senate members in debate on the bill relating to it.

Meanwhile our persistence has paid off in another area.

After receiving numerous complaints of snapped or locked clutch cables on International Harvester Scouts (1970 and 1971 models) we have urged the company to recall the automobiles. Our request was abruptly refused; the company denied there was a problem. When we found that a service bulletin had been sent to dealers explaining how to repair the problem that IH said did not exist, we again asked for a recall. The company remarked that the problem was "mechanical" not "safety." Imagine driving at high speeds on an expressway when your clutch cable snaps? We then organized a "nation-wide" picket of IH distributors and dealers utilizing groups in Fort Wayne, San Francisco and elsewhere. Within four days, the Federal Department of Transportation, until that time unwilling to launch a formal investigation of the matter, had begun a formal probe.

Just as we had done in Wallingford in 1971, we have uncovered facts and statistics on a "tax dodge" by a major corporation in a small Connecticut town. In the assessor's files in the small town of Middlebury, Uniroyal, the owners of a large tract and research center there, claimed a total value of $17 million for the property. But in the files of the Insurance Department (since the Uniroyal property is owned by Metropolitan Life Insurance Co. in New York), the whole property is supposedly worth $42 million. After speaking with an architect who had worked on the plant, the $42 million figure was confirmed. We then charged Uniroyal with a tax dodge of nearly $500,000.

We held a press conference in Middlebury with town residents who had been battling the Uniroyal assessment for years without ever having received substantial publicity. After making statements on the steps of the Town Hall, a cavalcade wound its way through lovely country roads to the Uniroyal plant where a "bill" for that amount was tacked on the large glass entrance doors.

The following week, the Board of Tax Review voted to bill Uniroyal for the amount of tax due.

The Uniroyal project prompted numerous phone calls from legislators, most of them simply offering congratulations, but others saying they would like to help us on future similar projects. One legislator told us that he had "some devastating figures" on another Uniroyal plant. Another suggested we join him in an effort at state-wide property tax reform.

Late one afternoon I received a call from a woman who said she was a legislative secretary. "Mr. Moffett? Please hold one moment," she said. "Who is it?" I asked. "One moment, please," she replied, ignoring my question.

A man's voice loudly exclaimed, "Mr. Moffett?" He was obviously trying to conceal his identity.

"Who is this?" I asked. Actually I should have known better since I regularly take calls where the callers don't want to reveal names.

"A state legislator," the voice replied. "I can't tell you my name, but I have some terrific information for you."

"Go ahead."

"Well, I think you did a great job on the Uniroyal thing. But I have some information on a corporation that will make Uniroyal look like child's play."

What he had was interesting indeed and thus still another project was spawned.

Appendix

THE QUESTIONNAIRES which follow are samples of the CCAG material used in the General Assembly Project. Where the questions related to specific Connecticut legislation, the wording has been changed slightly to make them more general.

The Legislative Interview Outline also included requests for position statements in the following areas: consumer protection, environment and pollution, tax structure, transportation, women's rights, civil rights and labor. The varying situations on these important issues in other states should determine the specific format of such questions for citizen groups in those states.

PRELIMINARY QUESTIONNAIRE FOR LEGISLATORS

NAME ....

ADDRESS...

PHONE LISTED? .... Yes............................No.............................

NUMBER (bus.)......................................(res.)..

List on separate sheets (one for you and one for your spouse) the following information;

A. OCCUPATION—list name of firm, agency, corporation, profession.

B. FIVE MAJOR CLIENTS OR ACCOUNTS (specifically five corporations and five individuals) OF YOUR FIRM, AGENCY, CORPORATION, OR PROFESSION—list in order of revenue to firm and include location.

C. SPECIFY TYPE OF PRACTICE OR BUSINESS:

—If corporation—position and areas of responsibility, and products sold.
—If independent insurance agent—specify type of insurance sold and corporations represented.
—If real estate agency—specify type of property most frequently bought or sold through your agency.

D. YEARLY INCOME—as stated in your 1971 and 1972 tax returns.

E. HOLDINGS AND AMOUNT—Itemize stocks in publicly held corporations, bonds, trusts, land owned. List all private corporations in which you either hold stock, or are an officer or member of the Board.

The following questions apply to the Legislator only:

F. COMMITTEE MEMBERSHIP

G. DO YOU HAVE REGULARLY SCHEDULED OFFICE HOURS FOR CONSTITUENTS? List times and frequency as well as location.

H. DO YOU PERIODICALLY MAIL A NEWSLETTER TO CONSTITUENTS? HOW OFTEN? PLEASE INCLUDE COPIES, IF AVAILABLE, WITH YOUR REPLY.

I. IN WHAT WAYS DO YOU KEEP YOUR CONSTITUENTS INFORMED ABOUT LEGISLATIVE ACTIVITIES AND OTHER IMPORTANT ISSUES?

J. LIST ORGANIZATIONS TO WHICH YOU BELONG, AND POSITIONS HELD. ALSO INCLUDE ANY AWARDS RECEIVED.

OPPONENT IN LAST CAMPAIGN ....

VOTING RESULTS (Use number of votes received by you and your opponent.)..

K. ENDORSEMENTS RECEIVED BY YOU—Include affiliation of any individuals.

L. ENDORSEMENTS RECEIVED BY YOUR OPPONENT—Include affiliation.

AMOUNT OF MONEY SPENT ON CAMPAIGN ....

WAS THERE A CAMPAIGN DEFICIT?............SURPLUS?............—fill in amount.

M. IF YOU BORROWED MONEY FOR YOUR CAMPAIGN, PLEAST LIST THE CREDITORS AND THE AMOUNTS LOANED.

N. LARGEST CONTRIBUTORS TO YOUR CAMPAIGN—Please list names, addresses, and corporate, union, organizational affiliations as well as amounts.

WHO WAS YOUR CAMPAIGN CHAIRMAN OR CHAIRWOMAN? ....
PAID?...................NONPAID?.....................IF DONATED, BY WHOM? ....

EMPLOYER ....

WHO WAS YOUR CAMPAIGN TREASURER?—specify occupation and employer. ....

PAID?...................NONPAID?.....................IF DONATED, BY WHOM? ....

O. WHICH CONTRIBUTORS, IF ANY, GAVE TO BOTH YOU AND YOUR OPPONENT?

P. LIST ALL COMMITTEES ESTABLISHED TO COLLECT FUNDS FOR YOUR CAMPAIGN.

CAMPAIGN LITERATURE AND ADVERTISEMENTS. IF POSSIBLE, WOULD YOU SEND US COPIES OF THIS MATERIAL? IF THIS IS NOT POSSIBLE, WILL YOU MAKE IT AVAILABLE TO US?

CITIZEN QUESTIONNAIRE

This questionnaire is an important part of the General Assembly Project since it will help to determine how well a legislator is serving the needs of his or her constituents. Since we could not possibly mass mail this document, we are relying on citizens and the press to see that as many people as possible know about the Project and have the opportunity to comment.

NAME (optional) ....
CITY OR TOWN..
Your Representative (state) ....

Your Senator (state)..

IF YOU WISH TO CONTACT YOUR LEGISLATOR, HOW DO YOU CONTACT
HIM OR HER?
Office hours?
Telephone?
Go to legislator's home?
Write a letter?
Send a telegram?
Other means..

WHAT DO YOU CONSIDER TO BE THE THREE MOST IMPORTANT PROBLEMS
IN YOUR AREA? ....

WHAT DO YOU THINK YOUR LEGISLATOR HAS DONE ABOUT THESE PROBLEMS?
(Be specific for both your representative and your senator if possible.)

DO YOU KNOW HOW YOUR LEGISLATORS HAVE VOTED ON CONSUMER,
ENVIRONMENTAL AND HUMAN RIGHTS ISSUES?

HOW CAN YOU FIND OUT HOW EACH LEGISLATOR VOTED? ....

COULD YOU DESCRIBE ANY SITUATIONS IN WHICH YOU HAVE DEALT WITH
YOUR LEGISLATOR? (We are interested only in situations which concern
important issues.)

FROM WHAT GROUPS OR INDIVIDUALS WITHIN OR OUTSIDE YOUR COMMUNITY
DO YOU THINK YOUR LEGISLATOR RECEIVES THE MOST ADVICE? (Answer
separately for each person, both representative and senator.)

LEGISLATIVE INTERVIEW OUTLINE

I. General Topics

1. What do you see as the central duties and responsibilities of a
state legislator? What qualities do you believe an individual must
possess in order to accomplish these purposes?

2. Whom do you respect most among your fellow legislators—choosing
some examples? Give reasons.

3. What has personally disappointed you most in the General Assembly,
either a single event or an unremedied condition?

4. What do you view as the most important bills you've sponsored
or co-sponsored? Why?

5. How do you decide to sponsor a particular bill or to not sponsor
another?

6. How do you allocate your time between your employment and

your duties as a state legislator? Does this present any difficulties for you?

7. We understand that the term "conflicts of interest" is both controversial and hard to define. But we would like to get an idea of what the term means to you. Could you give us your definition? In particular, have you ever encountered what you thought to be a real or potential conflict situation relating to you as a legislator? If so, how did you resolve it?

8. Are there any circumstances under which you would refuse a campaign contribution? Have you actually ever refused a contribution? (Use probes as appropriate to obtain specifics.)

9. How do you communicate your views and actions to your constituents? Do you have a periodic newsletter? A newspaper column (which paper?)? Do you issue press releases? (About how often? Are copies available?)

10. In what ways do you make yourself available to constituents who have complaints, criticisms, questions or ideas to express? Regular office hours (How often? Are they advertised?) What, if any, new channels have you established for citizen participation? Community forums? Special town meetings?

11. In general, how do you prepare yourself to vote on an issue? From what sources do you usually obtain information? Do you use the library often, for example? How frequently do you rely on other legislators for information? On lobbyists?

II. *Legislative & Election Issues*

ISSUE AREA: Legislative Procedure

1. Some legislators favor roll-call votes on all bills. Others do not. How frequently do you feel there should be a roll-call vote? What are your reasons for this opinion?

2. The party caucus has been singled out as both a very effective and a very objectionable institution by different people. Does reform of the caucus process seem like a priority issue to you? Why?

3. Do you find significant pressure on members in the caucus to vote against their wishes? Is there too much or too little pressure to vote the party position?

4. Does the caucus apparatus decrease citizen participation in the decision-making process? If so, in what ways?

5. Do you believe that the legislature in general could be more open to citizen inputs or participation? In what ways?

6. In your view, what role should executive sessions play in committee

deliberations? What role do you believe they play at the present time? Do you find this acceptable?

7. Should executive session minutes and roll-call vote tallies be available to the public?

8. Should there be fewer executive sessions or is the present number acceptable? Why or why not?

9. Have you or other committee members ever been prevented from stating your opinions on a bill during committee sessions? Can you describe the situation?

10. Are bills ever reported out of committee without full debate and fair voting? Does this seem to be a serious problem?

11. Do you favor publishing attendance records of legislators in committees in the Legislative Journal?

12. Do you have too many committee assignments? If so, how many would be appropriate?

ISSUE AREA: Lobbying and Advocacy

1. (If your state) has legislation to regulate in some ways the activity of lobbyists, is enforcement of this legislation adequate, in your opinion? Why or why not?

2. What do you feel is the most effective lobby or lobbies in the General Assembly? How does it achieve its effectiveness? (Attempt to determine how legislator ranks labor, business, education, League of Women Voters, Common Cause, Citizens' Lobby.)

3. In what ways, if any, do you find lobbyists helpful?

4. Can you give us some examples of how pressures are brought to bear on you by lobbyists? Do you find specific tactics objectionable?

5. Do you make any distinction between a lobby for profit-making interests and a citizen lobby?

6. Should there be a difference in the way those two types of lobbies are regulated? Should, for example, they both be charged the same fee for the right to lobby? Do you feel that there should be any fee at all for non-profit groups to lobby? (Be sure respondent understands that we are *not* referring to tax-exempt groups which are forbidden by law from lobbying.)

ISSUE AREA: Leadership

1. How does the party leadership help inform you on certain issues?

2. Have you ever been retaliated against or threatened for disagreeing with party leadership?

3. Do you think that party leadership is too susceptible to pressure from lobbyists? Explain.

4. In general, do you feel that there is either too much or too little party leadership control in the General Assembly? Explain.

ISSUE AREA: Legislative Reforms

1. Do you believe that members of the General Assembly should have to publicly disclose their personal wealth and financial connections? Please explain. (Check your CCAG position on this one for some leads on probing questions.)

2. Applicants for federal civil service positions are required to divulge details of previous employment, salary, description of work and supervisors. Should prospective and present members of state legislatures be required to do the same publicly? Please explain.

3. (If your state's) General Assembly is not a full-time body, do you believe it should become one?

4. What salary level would you suggest for a full-time body?

5. Do you believe, if the present body has a part-time status, that the salaries are adequate?

6. I think you'll agree that legislative bodies have a responsibility to see that once laws are passed they are effectively and fairly implemented. Should each legislative committee responsible for a state agency be required to hold general oversight hearings, perhaps on an annual basis? In what other ways can the oversight function be performed? In what ways have you as a legislator attempted to perform it? (Look especially for answers, such as "I called hearings," "I asked for meetings with agency officials," "I wrote letters to agency heads.")

ISSUE AREA: Elections

1. Do you feel that the present make-up of the General Assembly adequately reflects the different social, racial and economic segments in the state?

2. In particular, would you like to see more representation from some particular groups such as production workers, teachers, minorities, women, ethnic groups? Explain reasons.

3. In your district in the last ten years or so, do you believe that it has become easier or harder for any given individual to become a candidate? Elaborate please.

4. Is it difficult for an average citizen to finance or otherwise enter a General Assembly campaign? If so, how can this situation be changed? Is it a high priority issue?

6. Is it possible, in your view, for the General Assembly to objectively reapportion itself? Are there any ways in which reapportionment problems and stalemates such as those Connecticut has been experiencing can be avoided?

7. What would be the major difficulties facing a person who wanted to challenge you in your district for your party's nomination? (Look especially for these answers: "nomination procedure," "party structure," "your friends in the party," "financial resources," "name familiarity among constituents," "your record.")

ISSUE AREA: Media

1. Do you feel that the media has treated the General Assembly fairly in its coverage? Explain.

2. Do you feel that the media has personally treated you fairly? If not, could you give examples? (Need not mention the particular paper or radio-TV station.)

3. Does the media, in your opinion, offer enough in-depth coverage of General Assembly activities? Explain.

ISSUE AREA: Executive Branch

1. How balanced do you feel the powers of the executive and legislative branches are at the present time? What branch holds more power? Why?

2. What kind of a role does the current governor play in passing or blocking legislation? Explain.

3. It is possible for a governor to weaken or dilute legislative intent by appointing to commissions, councils and boards which implement laws people who are unqualified or politically dependent upon those they are supposed to regulate. Would you favor reform of the procedures of appointment? If so, how?

4. Are there ways in which the public could have more control over gubernatorial appointments? How? Would you favor legislative "advise and consent" on all major appointments? Would you favor a citizens' review committee to approve appointments?

5. What qualifications should "public members" of such commissions possess?

OUTLINE FOR PROFILES

I. INTRODUCTION

1. How long has the legislator been in the General Assembly?
2. What are the major concerns of the people in his district?
3. In what way did the legislator respond to the preliminary questionnaire? Which questions were not answered? What specific reasons were given by the legislator for not answering?
4. What was the income range of the legislator?
5. What is the general overview of the legislator?
   a. give any stand on an issue which may stand out,
   b. the legislator's main concerns,
   c. general feelings of legislator on citizen participation.

II. SERVICE TO CONSTITUENTS

1. How does the legislator generally seem to respond to his or her constituents?
2. Did the legislator vote by his conscience or constituents?
3. What did the interviews with community leaders show you about the community's attitudes toward legislator?
4. How did the legislator attempt to communicate with constituents?
   a. newsletter;
   b. newspaper;
   c. office hours.
5. How did the legislator respond to local concerns and issues?
   a. Did his or her opinion change on certain issues as a result of pressure from constituents?
   b. Was the legislator informed on the local issues?
   c. Was the legislator visible to constituents, especially during crises?

III. PERFORMANCE IN LEGISLATURE

1. How involved generally was the legislator with the General Assembly process?
   a. Did the legislator speak on the floor of the House or Senate?
   b. Did the legislator speak at public hearings?
   c. Did the legislator sponsor many bills?
   d. Was the legislator present for role call votes during sessions?
   e. Did the legislator take an active roll in committees?
   f. Did the legislator have a good attendance record in committees?
2. Did the legislator exert independence in voting or did he or she vote the party line?
3. Has the legislator demonstrated real concern and knowledge of certain issues or has been uninformed?

Include in this section the following statistics:
1. the number of roll call votes missed out of total number;
2. number of committee meetings missed out of total;
3. number of public hearings attended out of total for his or her committee;
4. number of bills sponsored;
5. and number of times spoke during both sessions.

IV. VIEW OF LEGISLATURE

1. What is the attitude of the legislator toward legislative reforms as seen in:
   a. roll call votes;
   b. party caucus;
   c. executive sessions;
   d. lobbyists;
   e. leadership;
   f. public disclosure;
   g. full-time legislature;
   h. oversight function;
   i. citizen participation.
2. Does the legislator think reforms are necessary in election and campaign laws?
3. Does the legislator generally seem to be an advocate for legislative reform?

V. KNOWLEDGE ON ISSUES AND VOTING RECORD

1. Did the legislator generally seem to have a grasp of the issues?
2. Was the legislator well-informed on consumer issues (Be specific by including some of key consumer votes with explanation of vote)?
3. How did the legislator obtain information on issues?
4. Who does the legislator rely on for information?
5. What statements did the legislator make in transcripts, newspapers, or interviews that explain his/her position?

USE THIS SAME FORMAT FOR ENVIRONMENTAL, FISCAL, TRANSPORTATION, HUMAN RIGHTS AND LABOR ISSUES.